There is always *something left to love. And if you ain't learned that, you ain't learned nothing.*

A RAISIN IN THE SUN
Act Three

A RAISIN IN THE SUN

Lorraine Hansberry

with Connections

HOLT, RINEHART AND WINSTON
Harcourt Brace & Company
Austin • New York • Orlando • Atlanta • San Francisco
Boston • Dallas • Toronto • London

A Raisin in the Sun was first presented by Philip Rose and David J. Cogan at the Ethel Barrymore Theatre, New York City, March 11, 1959.

This edition of *A Raisin in the Sun* is published by Holt, Rinehart and Winston as part of the HRW Library.

Front cover: foreground image of Sidney Poitier and Ruby Dee by Photofest. *Background wrap image:* houses on the south side of Chicago, April 1, 1941. Hulton Getty/Liaison Agency.

HRW is a registered trademark licensed to Holt, Rinehart and Winston.

Printed in the United States of America

ISBN 0-03-055099-8   5 6 043 03 02

Contents

Lorraine Hansberry
(1930–1965)

Lorraine Hansberry grew up on Chicago's South Side, the youngest of four children. Her father was a successful businessman, and her family was wealthy by neighborhood standards. When Hansberry was eight, her father moved the family to a white neighborhood as a protest against restrictive covenants, which were used to keep African Americans and other groups from living in certain areas.

Hansberry was educated in Chicago's public schools and showed an early talent for writing and drawing. She wrote plays and short stories while she was in high school and later as a student at the University of Wisconsin and the Art Institute of Chicago.

When *A Raisin in the Sun* opened in 1959, it was an instant success. This play marked the beginning of a vigorous black theater movement, which became one of the most vital forces in the modern American theater.

> How to describe the effect *A Raisin in the Sun* had on most of us when it opened in 1959! There I was in Detroit's Cass Theater, a young man who had never seen anywhere a black man express all the things I felt but never had the courage to express. . . . The power of the play had made us all aware of our uniqueness as blacks and had encouraged us to pursue our dreams. Indeed, the play had confirmed that our dreams were possible.
>
> —Woodie King, Jr.

Lloyd Richards directed a superb cast, which included Sidney Poitier, Claudia McNeil, Diana Sands, Ruby Dee, and Louis

Gossett. The play was translated into thirty languages and won the New York Drama Critics' Circle Award. At twenty-nine, Lorraine Hansberry became the youngest person—and the first African American playwright—ever to win that award.

Lorraine Hansberry's second Broadway play, *The Sign in Sidney Brustein's Window,* opened just three months before she died of cancer, at the age of thirty-four. *To Be Young, Gifted and Black,* a collection of letters, journal entries, speeches, and play excerpts, was published in 1969 and adapted for the stage that same year.

Hansberry's vitality and passionate commitment to others are reflected in these remarks, which she made two weeks before *A Raisin in the Sun* opened:

> I wish to live because life has within it that which is good, that which is beautiful, and that which is love. Therefore, since I have known all of these things, I have found them to be reason enough and—I wish to live. Moreover, because this is so, I wish others to live for generations and generations and generations and generations.

A RAISIN IN THE SUN

by
Lorraine Hansberry

A RAISIN IN THE SUN

What happens to a dream deferred?

    Does it dry up
    like a raisin in the sun?
    Or fester like a sore—
    And then run?
    Does it stink like rotten meat?
    Or crust and sugar over—
    like a syrupy sweet?

    Maybe it just sags
    like a heavy load.

    Or does it explode?

                —Langston Hughes

Characters

(In order of appearance)

Ruth Younger
Travis Younger
Walter Lee Younger (Brother)
Beneatha Younger
Lena Younger (Mama)
Joseph Asagai
George Murchison
Mrs. Johnson
Karl Lindner
Bobo
Moving Men

The action of the play is set in Chicago's South Side, sometime between World War II and the present.

Act One

Scene 1. Friday morning.
Scene 2. The following morning.

Act Two

Scene 1. Later, the same day.
Scene 2. Friday night, a few weeks later.
Scene 3. Moving day, one week later.

Act Three

An hour later.

Act One

Scene 1

The YOUNGER *living room would be a comfortable and well-ordered room if it were not for a number of indestructible contradictions to this state of being. Its furnishings are typical and undistinguished and their primary feature now is that they have clearly had to accommodate the living of too many people for too many years—and they are tired. Still, we can see that at some time, a time probably no longer remembered by the family (except perhaps for* MAMA), *the furnishings of this room were actually selected with care and love and even hope— and brought to this apartment and arranged with taste and pride.*

That was a long time ago. Now the once loved pattern of the couch upholstery has to fight to show itself from under acres of crocheted doilies and couch covers which have themselves finally come to be more important than the upholstery. And here a table or a chair has been moved to disguise the worn places in the carpet; but the carpet has fought back by showing its weariness, with depressing uniformity, elsewhere on its surface.

Weariness has, in fact, won in this room. Everything has been polished, washed, sat on, used, scrubbed too often. All pretenses but living itself have long since vanished from the very atmosphere of this room.

Moreover, a section of this room, for it is not really a room unto itself, though the landlord's lease would make it seem so, slopes backward to provide a small kitchen area, where the family prepares the meals that are eaten in the living room proper, which must also serve as dining room. The single window that has been provided for these "two" rooms is located in this kitchen area. The sole natural light the family may enjoy in the course of a day is only that which fights its way through this little window.

At left, a door leads to a bedroom which is shared by MAMA *and her daughter,* BENEATHA. *At right, opposite, is a second room (which in the beginning of the life of this apartment was probably a breakfast room) which serves as a bedroom for* WALTER *and his wife,* RUTH.

Time: Sometime between World War II and the present.

Place: Chicago's South Side.

At rise: It is morning dark in the living room. TRAVIS *is asleep on the make-down bed at center. An alarm clock sounds from within the bedroom at right, and presently* RUTH *enters from that room and closes the door behind her. She crosses sleepily toward the window. As she passes her sleeping son she reaches down and shakes him a little. At the window she raises the shade and a dusky South Side morning light comes in feebly. She fills a pot with water and puts it on to boil. She calls to the boy, between yawns, in a slightly muffled voice.*

RUTH *is about thirty. We can see that she was a pretty girl, even exceptionally so, but now it is apparent that life has been little that she expected, and disappointment has already begun to hang in her face. In a few years, before thirty-five even, she will be known among her people as a "settled woman."*

She crosses to her son and gives him a good, final, rousing shake.

Ruth. Come on now, boy, it's seven-thirty! (*Her son sits up at last, in a stupor of sleepiness.*) I say hurry up, Travis! You ain't the only person in the world got to use a bathroom! (*The child, a sturdy, handsome little boy of ten or eleven, drags himself out of the bed and almost blindly takes his towels and "today's clothes" from drawers and a closet and goes out to the bathroom, which is in an outside hall and which is shared by another family or families on the same floor.* RUTH *crosses to the bedroom door at right and opens it and calls in to her husband.*) Walter Lee! . . . It's after seven-thirty! Lemme see you do some waking up in there now! (*She waits.*) You better get up from there, man! It's after seven-thirty I tell you. (*She waits again.*) All right, you just go ahead and lay there and next thing you know Travis be finished and Mr. Johnson'll be in there and you'll be fussing and cussing round here like a madman! And be late too! (*She waits, at the end of patience.*) Walter Lee—it's time for you to GET UP!

[*She waits another second and then starts to go into the bedroom, but is apparently satisfied that her husband has begun to get up. She stops, pulls the door to, and returns to the kitchen area. She wipes her face with a moist cloth and runs her fingers through her sleep-disheveled hair in a vain effort and ties an apron around her house-coat. The bedroom door at right opens and her husband stands in the doorway in his pajamas, which are rumpled and mismated. He is a lean, intense young man in his middle thirties, inclined to quick nervous movements and erratic speech habits—and always in his voice there is a quality of indictment.*]

Walter. Is he out yet?

Ruth. What you mean *out*? He ain't hardly got in there good yet.

Walter (*wandering in, still more oriented to sleep than to a new day*). Well, what was you doing all that yelling for if I can't even get in there yet? (*Stopping and thinking*) Check coming today?

Ruth. They *said* Saturday and this is just Friday and I hopes to God you ain't going to get up here first thing this morning and start talking to me 'bout no money—'cause I 'bout don't want to hear it.

Walter. Something the matter with you this morning?

Ruth. No—I'm just sleepy as the devil. What kind of eggs you want?

Walter. Not scrambled. (RUTH *starts to scramble eggs.*) Paper come? (RUTH *points impatiently to the rolled up* Tribune *on the table, and he gets it and spreads it out and vaguely reads the front page.*) Set off another bomb yesterday.

Ruth (*maximum indifference*). Did they?

Walter (*looking up*). What's the matter with you?

Ruth. Ain't nothing the matter with me. And don't keep asking me that this morning.

Walter. Ain't nobody bothering you. (*Reading the news of the day absently again*) Say Colonel McCormick is sick.

Ruth (*affecting tea-party interest*). Is he now? Poor thing.

Walter (*sighing and looking at his watch*). Oh, me. (*He waits.*) Now what is that boy doing in that bathroom all this time? He just going to have to start getting up earlier. I can't be being late to work on account of him fooling around in there.

Ruth (*turning on him*). Oh, no he ain't going to be getting up no earlier no such thing! It ain't his fault that he can't get to bed no earlier nights 'cause he got a bunch of crazy good-for-nothing clowns sitting up running their mouths in what is supposed to be his bedroom after ten o'clock at night . . .

Walter. That's what you mad about, ain't it? The things I want to talk about with my friends just couldn't be important in your mind, could they?

[*He rises and finds a cigarette in her handbag on the table and crosses to the little window and looks out, smoking and deeply enjoying this first one.*]

Ruth (*almost matter-of-factly, a complaint too automatic to deserve emphasis*). Why you always got to smoke before you eat in the morning?

Walter (*at the window*). Just look at 'em down there . . . Running and racing to work . . . (*He turns and faces his wife and watches her a moment at the stove, and then, suddenly*) You look young this morning, baby.

Ruth (*indifferently*). Yeah?

Walter. Just for a second—stirring them eggs. Just for a second it was—you looked real young again. (*He reaches for her; she crosses away. Then, drily*) It's gone now—you look like yourself again!

Ruth. Man, if you don't shut up and leave me alone.

Walter (*looking out to the street again*). First thing a man ought to learn in life is not to talk love to no colored woman first thing in the morning. You all some eeeevil people at eight o'clock in the morning.

[TRAVIS *appears in the hall doorway, almost fully dressed and quite wide awake now, his towels and pajamas across his shoulders. He opens the door and signals for his father to make the bathroom in a hurry.*]

Travis (*watching the bathroom*). Daddy, come on!

[WALTER *gets his bathroom utensils and flies out to the bathroom.*]

Ruth. Sit down and have your breakfast, Travis.

Travis. Mama, this is Friday. (*Gleefully*) Check coming tomorrow, huh?

Ruth. You get your mind off money and eat your breakfast.

Travis (*eating*). This is the morning we supposed to bring the fifty cents to school.

Ruth. Well, I ain't got no fifty cents this morning.

Travis. Teacher say we have to.

Ruth. I don't care what teacher say. I ain't got it. Eat your breakfast, Travis.

Travis. I *am* eating.

Ruth. Hush up now and just eat!

[*The boy gives her an exasperated look for her lack of understanding, and eats grudgingly.*]

Travis. You think Grandmama would have it?

Ruth. No! And I want you to stop asking your grandmother for money, you hear me?

Travis (*outraged*). Gaaaleee! I don't ask her, she just gimme it sometimes!

Ruth. Travis Willard Younger—I got too much on me this morning to be—

Travis. Maybe Daddy—

Ruth. *Travis!*

[*The boy hushes abruptly. They are both quiet and tense for several seconds.*]

Travis (*presently*). Could I maybe go carry some groceries in front of the supermarket for a little while after school then?

Ruth. Just hush, I said. (TRAVIS *jabs his spoon into his cereal bowl viciously, and rests his head in anger upon his fists.*) If you through eating, you can get over there and make up your bed.

[*The boy obeys stiffly and crosses the room, almost mechanically, to the bed and more or less folds the bedding into a heap, then angrily gets his books and cap.*]

Travis (*sulking and standing apart from her unnaturally*). I'm gone.

Ruth (*looking up from the stove to inspect him automatically*). Come here. (*He crosses to her and she studies his head.*) If you don't take this comb and fix this here head, you better! (TRAVIS *puts down his books with a great sigh of oppression, and crosses to the mirror. His mother mutters under her breath about his "slubbornness."*) 'Bout to march out of here with that head looking just like chickens slept in it! I just don't know where you get your slubborn ways . . . And get your jacket, too. Looks chilly out this morning.

Travis (*with conspicuously brushed hair and jacket*). I'm gone.

Ruth. Get carfare and milk money—(*waving one finger*)—and not a single penny for no caps, you hear me?

Travis (*with sullen politeness*). Yes'm.

[*He turns in outrage to leave. His mother watches after him as in his frustration he approaches the door almost comically. When she speaks to him, her voice has become a very gentle tease.*]

Ruth (*mocking; as she thinks he would say it*). Oh, Mama makes me so mad sometimes, I don't know what to do! (*She waits and continues to his back as he stands stock-still in front of the door.*) I wouldn't kiss that woman goodbye for nothing in this world this morning! (*The boy finally turns around and rolls his eyes at her, knowing the mood has changed and he is vindicated; he does not, however, move toward her yet.*) Not for nothing in this world! (*She finally laughs aloud at him and holds out her arms to him and we see that it is a way between them, very old and practiced. He crosses to her and allows her to embrace him warmly but keeps his face fixed with masculine rigidity. She holds him back from her presently and looks at him and runs her fingers over the features of his face. With utter gentleness—*) Now—whose little old angry man are you?

Travis (*The masculinity and gruffness start to fade at last.*). Aw gaalee—Mama . . .

Ruth (*mimicking*). Aw—gaaaaalleeeee, Mama! (*She pushes him, with rough playfulness and finality, toward the door.*) Get on out of here or you going to be late.

Travis (*in the face of love, new aggressiveness*). Mama, could I *please* go carry groceries?

Ruth. Honey, it's starting to get so cold evenings.

Walter (*coming in from the bathroom and drawing a make-believe gun from a make-believe holster and shooting at his son*). What is it he wants to do?

Ruth. Go carry groceries after school at the supermarket.

Walter. Well, let him go . . .

Travis (*quickly, to the ally*). I *have* to—she won't gimme the fifty cents . . .

Walter (*to his wife only*). Why not?

Ruth (*simply, and with flavor*). 'Cause we don't have it.

Walter (*to* RUTH *only*). What you tell the boy things like that for? (*Reaching down into his pants with a rather important gesture*) Here, son—

[*He hands the boy the coin, but his eyes are directed to his wife's.* TRAVIS *takes the money happily.*]

Travis. Thanks, Daddy.

[*He starts out.* RUTH *watches both of them with murder in her eyes.* WALTER *stands and stares back at her with defiance, and suddenly reaches into his pocket again on an afterthought.*]

Walter (*without even looking at his son, still staring hard at his wife*). In fact, here's another fifty cents . . . Buy yourself some fruit today—or take a taxicab to school or something!

Travis. Whoopee—

[*He leaps up and clasps his father around the middle with his legs, and they face each other in mutual appreciation; slowly* WALTER LEE *peeks around the boy to catch the violent rays from his wife's eyes and draws his head back as if shot.*]

Walter. You better get down now—and get to school, man.

Travis (*at the door*). O.K. Goodbye.

[*He exits.*]

Walter (*after him, pointing with pride*). That's *my* boy. (*She looks at him in disgust and turns back to her work.*) You know what I was thinking 'bout in the bathroom this morning?

Ruth. No.

Walter. How come you always try to be so pleasant!

Ruth. What is there to be pleasant 'bout!

Walter. You want to know what I was thinking 'bout in the bathroom or not!

Ruth. I know what you thinking 'bout.

Walter (*ignoring her*). 'Bout what me and Willy Harris was talking about last night.

Ruth (*immediately—a refrain*). Willy Harris is a good-for-nothing loudmouth.

Walter. Anybody who talks to me has got to be a good-for-nothing loudmouth, ain't he? And what you know about who is just a good-for-nothing loudmouth? Charlie Atkins was just a "good-for-nothing loudmouth" too, wasn't he! When he wanted me to go in the dry-cleaning business with him. And now—he's grossing a hundred thousand a year. A hundred thousand dollars a year! You still call *him* a loudmouth!

Ruth (*bitterly*). Oh, Walter Lee . . .

[*She folds her head on her arms over the table.*]

Walter (*rising and coming to her and standing over her*). You tired, ain't you? Tired of everything. Me, the boy, the way we live—this beat-up hole—everything. Ain't you? (*She doesn't look up, doesn't answer.*) So tired—moaning and groaning all the time, but you wouldn't do nothing to help, would you? You couldn't be on my side that long for nothing, could you?

Ruth. Walter, please leave me alone.

Walter. A man needs for a woman to back him up . . .

Ruth. Walter—

Walter. Mama would listen to you. You know she listen to you more than she do me and Bennie. She think more of you. All you have to do is just sit down with her when you drinking your coffee one morning and talking 'bout things like you do and—(*He sits down beside her and demonstrates graphically what he thinks her methods and tone should be.*)—you just sip your coffee, see, and say easy like that you been thinking 'bout that deal Walter Lee is so interested in, 'bout the store and all, and sip

some more coffee, like what you saying ain't really that important to you—And the next thing you know, she be listening
good and asking you questions and when I come home—I can
tell her the details. This ain't no fly-by-night proposition, baby.
I mean we figured it out, me and Willy and Bobo.

Ruth (*with a frown*). Bobo?

Walter. Yeah. You see, this little liquor store we got in mind cost
seventy-five thousand and we figured the initial investment on
the place be 'bout thirty thousand, see. That be ten thousand
each. Course, there's a couple of hundred you got to pay so's
you don't spend your life just waiting for them clowns to let
your license get approved—

Ruth. You mean graft?

Walter (*frowning impatiently*). Don't call it that. See there, that
just goes to show you what women understand about the
world. Baby, don't *nothing* happen for you in this world 'less
you pay *somebody* off!

Ruth. Walter, leave me alone! (*She raises her head and stares at
him vigorously—then says, more quietly*) Eat your eggs, they
gonna be cold.

Walter (*straightening up from her and looking off*). That's it. There
you are. Man say to his woman: I got me a dream. His woman
say: Eat your eggs. (*Sadly, but gaining in power*) Man say: I got to
take hold of this here world, baby! And a woman will say: Eat
your eggs and go to work. (*Passionately now*) Man say: I got to
change my life, I'm choking to death, baby! And his woman
say—(*in utter anguish as he brings his fists down on his thighs*)—
Your eggs is getting cold!

Ruth (*softly*). Walter, that ain't none of our money.

Walter (*not listening at all or even looking at her*). This morning, I
was lookin' in the mirror and thinking about it . . . I'm thirty-
five years old; I been married eleven years and I got a boy who
sleeps in the living room—(*very, very quietly*)—and all I got to
give him is stories about how rich white people live . . .

Ruth. Eat your eggs, Walter.

Walter (*slams the table and jumps up*).—DAMN MY EGGS—
DAMN ALL THE EGGS THAT EVER WAS!

Ruth. Then go to work.

Walter (*looking up at her*). See—I'm trying to talk to you 'bout myself—(*shaking his head with the repetition*)—and all you can say is eat them eggs and go to work.

Ruth (*wearily*). Honey, you never say nothing new. I listen to you every day, every night and every morning, and you never say nothing new. (*Shrugging*) So you would rather *be* Mr. Arnold than be his chauffeur. So—I would *rather* be living in Buckingham Palace.

Walter. That is just what is wrong with the colored woman in this world . . . Don't understand about building their men up and making 'em feel like they somebody. Like they can do something.

Ruth (*drily, but to hurt*). There *are* colored men who do things.

Walter. No thanks to the colored woman.

Ruth. Well, being a colored woman, I guess I can't help myself none.

[*She rises and gets the ironing board and sets it up and attacks a huge pile of rough-dried clothes, sprinkling them in preparation for the ironing and then rolling them into tight fat balls.*]

Walter (*mumbling*). We one group of men tied to a race of women with small minds!

[*His sister* BENEATHA *enters. She is about twenty, as slim and intense as her brother. She is not as pretty as her sister-in-law, but her lean, almost intellectual face has a handsomeness of its own. She wears a bright-red flannel nightie, and her thick hair stands wildly about her head. Her speech is a mixture of many things; it is different from the rest of the family's insofar as education has permeated her sense of English—and perhaps the Midwest rather than the South has finally—at last—won out in her inflection; but not altogether, because over all of it is a soft slurring and transformed use of vowels which is the decided influence of the South Side. She passes through the room without looking at either* RUTH *or* WALTER *and goes to the outside door and looks, a little blindly, out to the bathroom. She sees that it has been lost to the Johnsons. She closes the door with a sleepy vengeance and crosses to the table and sits down a little defeated.*]

Beneatha. I am going to start timing those people.

Walter. You should get up earlier.

Beneatha (*her face in her hands. She is still fighting the urge to go back to bed.*). Really—would you suggest dawn? Where's the paper?

Walter (*pushing the paper across the table to her as he studies her almost clinically, as though he has never seen her before*). You a horrible-looking chick at this hour.

Beneatha (*drily*). Good morning, everybody.

Walter (*senselessly*). How is school coming?

Beneatha (*in the same spirit*). Lovely. Lovely. And you know, biology is the greatest. (*Looking up at him*) I dissected something that looked just like you yesterday.

Walter. I just wondered if you've made up your mind and everything.

Beneatha (*gaining in sharpness and impatience*). And what did I answer yesterday morning—and the day before that?

Ruth (*from the ironing board, like someone disinterested and old*). Don't be so nasty, Bennie.

Beneatha (*still to her brother*). And the day before that and the day before that!

Walter (*defensively*). I'm interested in you. Something wrong with that? Ain't many girls who decide—

Walter *and* **Beneatha** (*in unison*). —"to be a doctor."

[*Silence*]

Walter. Have we figured out yet just exactly how much medical school is going to cost?

Ruth. Walter Lee, why don't you leave that girl alone and get out of here to work?

Beneatha (*exits to the bathroom and bangs on the door*). Come on out of there, please!

[*She comes back into the room.*]

Walter (*looking at his sister intently*). You know the check is coming tomorrow.

Beneatha (*turning on him with a sharpness all her own*). That money belongs to Mama, Walter, and it's for her to decide how she wants to use it. I don't care if she wants to buy a house or a rocket ship or just nail it up somewhere and look at it. It's hers. Not ours—*hers.*

Walter (*bitterly*). Now ain't that fine! You just got your mother's interest at heart, ain't you, girl? You such a nice girl—but if Mama got that money she can always take a few thousand and help you through school too—can't she?

Beneatha. I have never asked anyone around here to do anything for me!

Walter. No! And the line between asking and just accepting when the time comes is big and wide—ain't it!

Beneatha (*with fury*). What do you want from me, Brother—that I quit school or just drop dead, which!

Walter. I don't want nothing but for you to stop acting holy 'round here. Me and Ruth done made some sacrifices for you—why can't you do something for the family?

Ruth. Walter, don't be dragging me in it.

Walter. You are in it—Don't you get up and go work in somebody's kitchen for the last three years to help put clothes on her back?

Ruth. Oh, Walter—that's not fair . . .

Walter. It ain't that nobody expects you to get on your knees and say thank you, Brother; thank you, Ruth; thank you, Mama—and thank you, Travis, for wearing the same pair of shoes for two semesters—

Beneatha (*dropping to her knees*). Well—I *do*—all right?—thank everybody! And forgive me for ever wanting to be anything at all! (*Pursuing him on her knees across the floor*) FORGIVE ME, FORGIVE ME, FORGIVE ME!

Ruth. Please stop it! Your mama'll hear you.

Walter. What fool told you you had to be a doctor? If you so crazy 'bout messing 'round with sick people—then go be a nurse like other women—or just get married and be quiet . . .

Beneatha. Well—you finally got it said . . . It took you three years but you finally got it said. Walter, give up; leave me alone—it's Mama's money.

Walter. *He was my father, too!*

Beneatha. So what? He was mine, too—and Travis' grand-father—but the insurance money belongs to Mama. Picking on me is not going to make her give it to you to invest in any liquor stores—(*underbreath, dropping into a chair*)—and I for one say, God bless Mama for that!

Walter (*to* RUTH). See—did you hear? Did you hear!

Ruth. Honey, please go to work.

Walter. Nobody in this house is ever going to understand me.

Beneatha. Because you're a nut.

Walter. Who's a nut?

Beneatha. You—you are a nut. Thee is mad, boy.

Walter (*looking at his wife and his sister from the door, very sadly*). The world's most backward race of people, and that's a fact.

Beneatha (*turning slowly in her chair*). And then there are all those prophets who would lead us out of the wilderness— (WALTER *slams out of the house.*)—into the swamps!

Ruth. Bennie, why you always gotta be pickin' on your brother? Can't you be a little sweeter sometimes? (*Door opens.* WALTER *walks in. He fumbles with his cap, starts to speak, clears throat, looks everywhere but at* RUTH. *Finally:*)

Walter (*to* RUTH). I need some money for carfare.

Ruth (*looks at him, then warms; teasing, but tenderly*). Fifty cents? (*She goes to her bag and gets money.*) Here—take a taxi!

[WALTER *exits.* MAMA *enters. She is a woman in her early sixties, full-bodied and strong. She is one of those women of a certain grace and beauty who wear it so unobtrusively that it takes a while to notice. Her dark-brown face is surrounded by the total whiteness of her hair, and, being a woman who has adjusted to many things in life and over-come many more, her face is full of strength. She has, we can see, wit and faith of a kind that keep her eyes lit and full of interest and expectancy. She is, in a word, a beautiful woman. Her bearing is per-haps most like the noble bearing of the women of the Hereros of South West Africa—rather as if she imagines that as she walks she still bears a basket or a vessel upon her head. Her speech, on the other hand, is as careless as her carriage is precise—she is inclined to slur every-thing—but her voice is perhaps not so much quiet as simply soft.*]

Mama. Who that 'round here slamming doors at this hour?

[*She crosses through the room, goes to the window, opens it, and brings in a feeble little plant growing doggedly in a small pot on the windowsill. She feels the dirt and puts it back out.*]

Ruth. That was Walter Lee. He and Bennie was at it again.

Mama. My children and they tempers. Lord, if this little old plant don't get more sun than it's been getting it ain't never going to see spring again. (*She turns from the window.*) What's the matter with you this morning, Ruth? You looks right peaked. You aiming to iron all them things? Leave some for me. I'll get to 'em this afternoon. Bennie honey, it's too drafty for you to be sitting 'round half dressed. Where's your robe?

Beneatha. In the cleaners.

Mama. Well, go get mine and put it on.

Beneatha. I'm not cold, Mama, honest.

Mama. I know—but you so thin . . .

Beneatha (*irritably*). Mama, I'm not cold.

Mama (*seeing the make-down bed as* TRAVIS *has left it*). Lord have mercy, look at that poor bed. Bless his heart—he tries, don't he?

[*She moves to the bed* TRAVIS *has sloppily made up.*]

Ruth. No—he don't half try at all 'cause he knows you going to come along behind him and fix everything. That's just how come he don't know how to do nothing right now—you done spoiled that boy so.

Mama (*folding bedding*). Well—he's a little boy. Ain't supposed to know 'bout housekeeping. My baby, that's what he is. What you fix for his breakfast this morning?

Ruth (*angrily*). I feed my son, Lena!

Mama. I ain't meddling—(*underbreath; busybodyish*) I just noticed all last week he had cold cereal, and when it starts getting this chilly in the fall a child ought to have some hot grits or something when he goes out in the cold—

Ruth (*furious*). I gave him hot oats—is that all right!

Mama. I ain't meddling. (*Pause*) Put a lot of nice butter on it? (RUTH *shoots her an angry look and does not reply.*) He likes lots of butter.

Ruth (*exasperated*). Lena—

Mama (*to* BENEATHA. MAMA *is inclined to wander conversationally sometimes.*). What was you and your brother fussing 'bout this morning?

Beneatha. It's not important, Mama.

[*She gets up and goes to look out at the bathroom, which is apparently free, and she picks up her towels and rushes out.*]

Mama. What was they fighting about?

Ruth. Now you know as well as I do.

Mama (*shaking her head*). Brother still worrying hisself sick about that money?

Ruth. You know he is.

Mama. You had breakfast?

Ruth. Some coffee.

Mama. Girl, you better start eating and looking after yourself better. You almost thin as Travis.

Ruth. Lena—

Mama. Un-hunh?

Ruth. What are you going to do with it?

Mama. Now don't you start, child. It's too early in the morning to be talking about money. It ain't Christian.

Ruth. It's just that he got his heart set on that store—

Mama. You mean that liquor store that Willy Harris want him to invest in?

Ruth. Yes—

Mama. We ain't no business people, Ruth. We just plain working folks.

Ruth. Ain't nobody business people till they go into business. Walter Lee say colored people ain't never going to start getting ahead till they start gambling on some different kinds of things in the world—investments and things.

Mama. What done got into you, girl? Walter Lee done finally sold you on investing.

Ruth. No. Mama, something is happening between Walter and me. I don't know what it is—but he needs something—something I can't give him any more. He needs this chance, Lena.

Mama (*frowning deeply*). But liquor, honey—

Ruth. Well—like Walter say—I spec people going to always be drinking themselves some liquor.

Mama. Well—whether they drinks it or not ain't none of my business. But whether I go into business selling it to 'em *is,* and I don't want that on my ledger this late in life. (*Stopping suddenly and studying her daughter-in-law*) Ruth Younger, what's the matter with you today? You look like you could fall over right there.

Ruth. I'm tired.

Mama. Then you better stay home from work today.

Ruth. I can't stay home. She'd be calling up the agency and screaming at them, "My girl didn't come in today—send me somebody! My girl didn't come in!" Oh, she just have a fit . . .

Mama. Well, let her have it. I'll just call her up and say you got the flu—

Ruth (*laughing*). Why the flu?

Mama. 'Cause it sounds respectable to 'em. Something white people get, too. They know 'bout the flu. Otherwise they think you been cut up or something when you tell 'em you sick.

Ruth. I got to go in. We need the money.

Mama. Somebody would of thought my children done all but starved to death the way they talk about money here late. Child, we got a great big old check coming tomorrow.

Ruth (*sincerely, but also self-righteously*). Now that's your money. It ain't got nothing to do with me. We all feel like that— Walter and Bennie and me—even Travis.

Mama (*thoughtfully, and suddenly very far away*). Ten thousand dollars—

Ruth. Sure is wonderful.

Mama. Ten thousand dollars.

Ruth. You know what you should do, Miss Lena? You should take yourself a trip somewhere. To Europe or South America or someplace—

Mama (*throwing up her hands at the thought*). Oh, child!

Ruth. I'm serious. Just pack up and leave! Go on away and enjoy yourself some. Forget about the family and have yourself a ball for once in your life—

Mama (*drily*). You sound like I'm just about ready to die. Who'd go with me? What I look like wandering 'round Europe by myself?

Ruth. Shoot—these here rich white women do it all the time. They don't think nothing of packing up they suitcases and piling on one of them big steamships and—swoosh!—they gone, child.

Mama. Something always told me I wasn't no rich white woman.

Ruth. Well—what are you going to do with it then?

Mama. I ain't rightly decided. (*Thinking. She speaks now with emphasis.*) Some of it got to be put away for Beneatha and her schoolin'—and ain't nothing going to touch that part of it. Nothing. (*She waits several seconds, trying to make up her mind about something, and looks at* RUTH *a little tentatively before going on.*) Been thinking that we maybe could meet the notes on a little old two-story somewhere, with a yard where Travis could play in the summertime, if we use part of the insurance for a down payment and everybody kind of pitch in. I could maybe take on a little day work again, few days a week—

Ruth (*studying her mother-in-law furtively and concentrating on her ironing, anxious to encourage without seeming to*). Well, Lord knows, we've put enough rent into this here rat trap to pay for four houses by now . . .

Mama (*looking up at the words "rat trap" and then looking around and leaning back and sighing—in a suddenly reflective mood—*). "Rat trap"—yes, that's all it is. (*Smiling*) I remember just as well the day me and Big Walter moved in here. Hadn't been married but two weeks and wasn't planning on living here no more than a year. (*She shakes her head at the dissolved dream.*) We was going to set away, little by little, don't you know, and buy a little place out in Morgan Park. We had even picked out the house. (*Chuckling a little*) Looks right dumpy today. But Lord, child, you should know all the dreams I had 'bout buying that house and fixing it up and making me a little garden in the back—(*She waits and stops smiling.*) And didn't none of it happen.

[*Dropping her hands in a futile gesture*]

Ruth (*keeps her head down, ironing*). Yes, life can be a barrel of disappointments, sometimes.

Mama. Honey, Big Walter would come in here some nights back then and slump down on that couch there and just look at the rug, and look at me and look at the rug and then back at me—and I'd know he was down then . . . really down. (*After a second very long and thoughtful pause; she is seeing back to times that only she can see.*) And then, Lord, when I lost that baby—little Claude—I almost thought I was going to lose Big Walter too. Oh, that man grieved hisself! He was one man to love his children.

Ruth. Ain't nothin' can tear at you like losin' your baby.

Mama. I guess that's how come that man finally worked hisself to death like he done. Like he was fighting his own war with this here world that took his baby from him.

Ruth. He sure was a fine man, all right. I always liked Mr. Younger.

Mama. Crazy 'bout his children! God knows there was plenty wrong with Walter Younger—hard-headed, mean, kind of wild with women—plenty wrong with him. But he sure loved his children. Always wanted them to have something—be something. That's where Brother gets all these notions, I reckon. Big Walter used to say, he'd get right wet in the eyes sometimes, lean his head back with the water standing in his eyes and say, "Seem like God didn't see fit to give the black man nothing but dreams—but He did give us children to make them dreams seem worth while." (*She smiles.*) He could talk like that, don't you know.

Ruth. Yes, he sure could. He was a good man, Mr. Younger.

Mama. Yes, a fine man—just couldn't never catch up with his dreams, that's all.

[BENEATHA *comes in, brushing her hair and looking up to the ceiling, where the sound of a vacuum cleaner has started up.*]

Beneatha. What could be so dirty on that woman's rugs that she has to vacuum them every single day?

Ruth. I wish certain young women 'round here who I could name would take inspiration about certain rugs in a certain apartment I could also mention.

Beneatha (*shrugging*). Well, good God, how much cleaning can a house need.

Mama (*not liking the Lord's name used thus*). Bennie!

Ruth. Just listen to her—just listen!

Beneatha. Oh, . . .

Mama. If you use the Lord's name just one more time—

Beneatha (*a bit of a whine*). Oh, Mama—

Ruth. Fresh—just fresh as salt, this girl!

Beneatha (*drily*). Well—if the salt loses its savor—

Mama. Now that will do. I just ain't going to have you 'round here reciting the scriptures in vain—you hear me?

Beneatha. How did I manage to get on everybody's wrong side by just walking into a room?

Ruth. If you weren't so fresh—

Beneatha. Ruth, I'm twenty years old.

Mama. What time you be home from school today?

Beneatha. Kind of late. (*With enthusiasm*) Madeline is going to start my guitar lessons today.

[MAMA *and* RUTH *look up with the same expression.*]

Mama. Your *what* kind of lessons?

Beneatha. Guitar.

Ruth. Oh, Father!

Mama. How come you done taken it in your mind to learn to play the guitar?

Beneatha. I just want to, that's all.

Mama (*smiling*). Lord, child, don't you know what to do with yourself? How long it going to be before you get tired of this now—like you got tired of that little play-acting group you joined last year? (*Looking at* RUTH) And what was it the year before that?

Ruth. The horseback-riding club for which she bought that fifty-five-dollar riding habit that's been hanging in the closet ever since!

Mama (*to* BENEATHA). Why you got to flit so from one thing to another, baby?

Beneatha (*sharply*). I just want to learn to play the guitar. Is there anything wrong with that?

Mama. Ain't nobody trying to stop you. I just wonders sometimes why you has to flit so from one thing to another all the time. You ain't never done nothing with all that camera equipment you brought home—

Beneatha. I don't flit! I—I experiment with different forms of expression—

Ruth. Like riding a horse?

Beneatha. —People have to express themselves one way or another.

Mama. What is it you want to express?

Beneatha (*angrily*). Me! (MAMA *and* RUTH *look at each other and burst into raucous laughter.*) Don't worry—I don't expect you to understand.

Mama (*to change the subject*). Who you going out with tomorrow night?

Beneatha (*with displeasure*). George Murchison again.

Mama (*pleased*). Oh—you getting a little sweet on him?

Ruth. You ask me, this child ain't sweet on nobody but herself—(*Underbreath*) Express herself!

[*They laugh.*]

Beneatha. Oh—I like George all right, Mama. I mean I like him enough to go out with him and stuff, but—

Ruth (*for devilment*). What does *and stuff* mean?

Beneatha. Mind your own business.

Mama. Stop picking at her now, Ruth. (*She chuckles—then a suspicious sudden look at her daughter as she turns in her chair for emphasis.*) What DOES it mean?

Beneatha (*wearily*). Oh, I just mean I couldn't ever really be serious about George. He's—he's so shallow.

Ruth. Shallow—what do you mean he's shallow? He's *Rich*!

Mama. Hush, Ruth.

Beneatha. I know he's rich. He knows he's rich, too.

Ruth. Well—what other qualities a man got to have to satisfy you, little girl?

Beneatha. You wouldn't even begin to understand. Anybody who married Walter could not possibly understand.

Mama (*outraged*). What kind of way is that to talk about your brother?

Beneatha. Brother is a flip—let's face it.

Mama (*to* RUTH, *helplessly*). What's a flip?

Ruth (*glad to add kindling*). She's saying he's crazy.

Beneatha. Not crazy. Brother isn't really crazy yet—he—he's an elaborate neurotic.

Mama. Hush your mouth!

Beneatha. As for George. Well. George looks good—he's got a beautiful car and he takes me to nice places and, as my sister-in-law says, he is probably the richest boy I will ever get to know and I even like him sometimes—but if the Youngers are sitting around waiting to see if their little Bennie is going to tie up the family with the Murchisons, they are wasting their time.

Ruth. You mean you wouldn't marry George Murchison if he asked you someday? That pretty, rich thing? Honey, I knew you was odd—

Beneatha. No I would not marry him if all I felt for him was what I feel now. Besides, George's family wouldn't really like it.

Mama. Why not?

Beneatha. Oh, Mama—The Murchisons are honest-to-God-real-*live*-rich colored people, and the only people in the world who are more snobbish than rich white people are rich colored people. I thought everybody knew that. I've met Mrs. Murchison. She's a scene!

Mama. You must not dislike people 'cause they well off, honey.

Beneatha. Why not? It makes just as much sense as disliking people 'cause they are poor, and lots of people do that.

Ruth (*a wisdom-of-the-ages manner. To* MAMA). Well, she'll get over some of this—

Beneatha. Get over it? What are you talking about, Ruth? Listen, I'm going to be a doctor. I'm not worried about who I'm going to marry yet—if I ever get married.

Mama *and* **Ruth.** *If!*

Mama. Now, Bennie—

Beneatha. Oh, I probably will . . . but first I'm going to be a doctor, and George, for one, still thinks that's pretty funny. I couldn't be bothered with that. I am going to be a doctor and everybody around here better understand that!

Mama (*kindly*). 'Course you going to be a doctor, honey, God willing.

Beneatha (*drily*). God hasn't got a thing to do with it.

Mama. Beneatha—that just wasn't necessary.

Beneatha. Well . . . I get sick of hearing about God.

Mama. Beneatha!

Beneatha. I mean it! I'm just tired of hearing about God all the time. What has He got to do with anything? Does he pay tuition?

Mama. You 'bout to get your fresh little jaw slapped!

Ruth. That's just what she needs, all right!

Beneatha. Why? Why can't I say what I want to around here, like everybody else?

Mama. It don't sound nice for a young girl to say things like that—you wasn't brought up that way. Me and your father went to trouble to get you and Brother to church every Sunday.

Beneatha. Mama, you don't understand. It's all a matter of ideas, and that is just one idea I don't accept. It's not important. I am not going out and be immoral or commit crimes because I don't believe in God. I don't even think about it. It's just that I get tired of Him getting credit for all the things the human race achieves through its own stubborn effort. There simply is no God—there is only man and it is *he* who makes miracles!

[MAMA *absorbs this speech, studies her daughter, and rises slowly and crosses to* BENEATHA *and slaps her powerfully across the face. After, there is only silence and the daughter drops her eyes from her mother's face, and* MAMA *is very tall before her.*]

Mama. Now—you say after me, in my mother's house there is still God. (*There is a long pause and* BENEATHA *stares at the floor wordlessly.* MAMA *repeats the phrase with precision and cool*

emotion.) In my mother's house there is still God.
Beneatha. In my mother's house there is still God.

[*A long pause*]

Mama (*walking away from* BENEATHA, *too disturbed for triumphant posture. Stopping and turning back to her daughter*). There are some ideas we ain't going to have in this house. Not long as I am at the head of this family.
Beneatha. Yes, ma'am.

[MAMA *walks out of the room.*]

Ruth (*almost gently, with profound understanding*). You think you a woman, Bennie—but you still a little girl. What you did was childish—so you got treated like a child.
Beneatha. I see. (*Quietly*) I also see that everybody thinks it's all right for Mama to be a tyrant. But all the tyranny in the world will never make her right!

[*She picks up her books and goes out. Pause.*]

Ruth (*goes to* MAMA'*s door*). She said she was sorry.
Mama (*coming out, going to her plant*). They frightens me, Ruth. My children.
Ruth. You got good children, Lena. They just a little off sometimes—but they're good.
Mama. No—there's something come down between me and them that don't let us understand each other and I don't know what it is. One done almost lost his mind thinking 'bout money all the time and the other done commence to talk about things I can't seem to understand in no form or fashion. What is it that's changing, Ruth?
Ruth (*soothingly, older than her years*). Now . . . you taking it all too seriously. You just got strong-willed children and it takes a strong woman like you to keep 'em in hand.
Mama (*looking at her plant and sprinkling a little water on it*). They spirited all right, my children. Got to admit they got spirit—Bennie and Walter. Like this little old plant that ain't never had enough sunshine or nothing—and look at it . . .

[*She has her back to* RUTH, *who has had to stop ironing and lean against something and put the back of her hand to her forehead.*]

Ruth (*trying to keep* MAMA *from noticing*). You . . . sure . . . loves that little old thing, don't you? . . .

Mama. Well, I always wanted me a garden like I used to see sometimes at the back of the houses down home. This plant is close as I ever got to having one. (*She looks out of the window as she replaces the plant.*) Lord, ain't nothing as dreary as the view from this window on a dreary day, is there? Why ain't you singing this morning, Ruth? Sing that "No Ways Tired." That song always lifts me up so—(*She turns at last to see that* RUTH *has slipped quietly to the floor, in a state of semiconsciousness.*) Ruth! Ruth honey—what's the matter with you . . . Ruth!

Curtain

Scene 2

It is the following morning; a Saturday morning, and housecleaning is in progress at the YOUNGERS. *Furniture has been shoved hither and yon and* MAMA *is giving the kitchen-area walls a washing down.* BENEATHA, *in dungarees, with a handkerchief tied around her face, is spraying insecticide into the cracks in the walls. As they work, the radio is on and a South Side disc-jockey program is inappropriately filling the house with a rather exotic saxophone blues.* TRAVIS, *the sole idle one, is leaning on his arms, looking out of the window.*

Travis. Grandmama, that stuff Bennie is using smells awful. Can I go downstairs, please?
Mama. Did you get all them chores done already? I ain't seen you doing much.
Travis. Yes'm—finished early. Where did Mama go this morning?
Mama (*looking at* BENEATHA). She had to go on a little errand.

[*The phone rings.* BENEATHA *runs to answer it and reaches it before* WALTER, *who has entered from bedroom.*]

Travis. Where?
Mama. To tend to her business.
Beneatha. Haylo . . . (*Disappointed*) Yes, he is. (*She tosses the phone to* WALTER, *who barely catches it.*) It's Willy Harris again.
Walter (*as privately as possible under* MAMA's *gaze*). Hello, Willy. Did you get the papers from the lawyer? . . . No, not yet. I told you the mailman doesn't get here till ten-thirty . . . No, I'll come there . . . Yeah! Right away. (*He hangs up and goes for his coat.*)
Beneatha. Brother, where did Ruth go?
Walter (*as he exits*). How should I know!
Travis. Aw come on, Grandma. Can I go outside?
Mama. Oh, I guess so. You stay right in front of the house, though, and keep a good lookout for the postman.
Travis. Yes'm. (*He darts into bedroom for stickball and bat, reenters, and sees* BENEATHA *on her knees spraying under sofa with behind upraised. He edges closer to the target, takes aim, and lets her have it. She screams.*) Leave them poor little cockroaches alone, they

ain't bothering you none! (*He runs as she swings the spray gun at him viciously and playfully.*) Grandma! Grandma!

Mama. Look out there, girl, before you be spilling some of that stuff on that child!

Travis (*safely behind the bastion of* MAMA). That's right—look out, now! (*He exits.*)

Beneatha (*drily*). I can't imagine that it would hurt him—it has never hurt the roaches.

Mama. Well, little boys' hides ain't as tough as South Side roaches. You better get over there behind the bureau. I seen one marching out of there like Napoleon yesterday.

Beneatha. There's really only one way to get rid of them, Mama—

Mama. How?

Beneatha. Set fire to this building! Mama, where did Ruth go?

Mama (*looking at her with meaning*). To the doctor, I think.

Beneatha. The doctor? What's the matter? (*They exchange glances.*) You don't think—

Mama (*with her sense of drama*). Now I ain't saying what I think. But I ain't never been wrong 'bout a woman neither.

[*The phone rings.*]

Beneatha (*at the phone*). Hay-lo . . . (*Pause, and a moment of recognition*) Well—when did you get back! . . . And how was it? . . . Of course I've missed you—in my way . . . This morning? No . . . housecleaning and all that and Mama hates it if I let people come over when the house is like this . . . You *have*? Well, that's different . . . What is it—Oh, what the heck, come on over . . . Right, see you then. *Arrivederci.*

[*She hangs up.*]

Mama (*who has listened vigorously, as is her habit*). Who is that you inviting over here with this house looking like this? You ain't got the pride you was born with!

Beneatha. Asagai doesn't care how houses look, Mama—he's an intellectual.

Mama. *Who?*

Beneatha. Asagai—Joseph Asagai. He's an African boy I met on campus. He's been studying in Canada all summer.
Mama. What's his name?
Beneatha. Asagai, Joseph. Ah-sah-guy . . . He's from Nigeria.
Mama. Oh, that's the little country that was founded by slaves way back . . .
Beneatha. No, Mama—that's Liberia.
Mama. I don't think I never met no African before.
Beneatha. Well, do me a favor and don't ask him a whole lot of ignorant questions about Africans. I mean, do they wear clothes and all that—
Mama. Well, now, I guess if you think we so ignorant 'round here maybe you shouldn't bring your friends here—
Beneatha. It's just that people ask such crazy things. All anyone seems to know about when it comes to Africa is Tarzan—
Mama (*indignantly*). Why should I know anything about Africa?
Beneatha. Why do you give money at church for the missionary work?
Mama. Well, that's to help save people.
Beneatha. You mean save them from *heathenism*—
Mama (*innocently*). Yes.
Beneatha. I'm afraid they need more salvation from the British and the French.

[RUTH *comes in forlornly and pulls off her coat with dejection. They both turn to look at her.*]

Ruth (*dispiritedly*). Well, I guess from all the happy faces—everybody knows.
Beneatha. You pregnant?
Mama. Lord have mercy, I sure hope it's a little old girl. Travis ought to have a sister.

[BENEATHA *and* RUTH *give her a hopeless look for this grandmotherly enthusiasm.*]

Beneatha. How far along are you?
Ruth. Two months.

Beneatha. Did you mean to? I mean did you plan it or was it an accident?

Mama. What do you know about planning or not planning?

Beneatha. Oh, Mama.

Ruth (*wearily*). She's twenty years old, Lena.

Beneatha. Did you plan it, Ruth?

Ruth. Mind your own business.

Beneatha. It is my business—where is he going to live, on the roof? (*There is silence following the remark as the three women react to the sense of it.*) Gee—I didn't mean that, Ruth, honest. Gee, I don't feel like that at all. I—I think it is wonderful.

Ruth (*dully*). Wonderful.

Beneatha. Yes—really.

Mama (*looking at* RUTH, *worried*). Doctor say everything going to be all right?

Ruth (*far away*). Yes—she says everything is going to be fine . . .

Mama (*immediately suspicious*). "She"—What doctor you went to?

[RUTH *folds over, near hysteria.*]

Mama (*worriedly hovering over* RUTH). Ruth honey—what's the matter with you—you sick?

[RUTH *has her fists clenched on her thighs and is fighting hard to suppress a scream that seems to be rising in her.*]

Beneatha. What's the matter with her, Mama?

Mama (*working her fingers in* RUTH'S *shoulders to relax her*). She be all right. Women gets right depressed sometimes when they get her way. (*Speaking softly, expertly, rapidly*) Now you just relax. That's right . . . just lean back, don't think 'bout nothing at all . . . nothing at all—

Ruth. I'm all right . . .

[*The glassy-eyed look melts and then she collapses into a fit of heavy sobbing. The bell rings.*]

Beneatha. Oh . . . that must be Asagai.

Mama (*to* RUTH). Come on now, honey. You need to lie down and rest awhile . . . then have some nice hot food.

[*They exit,* RUTH's *weight on her mother-in-law.* BENEATHA, *herself profoundly disturbed, opens the door to admit a rather dramatic-looking young man with a large package.*]

Asagai. Hello, Alaiyo—

Beneatha (*holding the door open and regarding him with pleasure*). Hello . . . (*Long pause*) Well—come in. And please excuse everything. My mother was very upset about my letting anyone come here with the place like this.

Asagai (*coming into the room*). You look disturbed too . . . Is something wrong?

Beneatha (*still at the door, absently*). Yes . . . we've all got acute ghetto-itus. (*She smiles and comes toward him, finding a cigarette and sitting.*) So—sit down! No! Wait! (*She whips the spray gun off sofa where she had left it and puts the cushions back. At last perches on arm of sofa. He sits.*) So, how was Canada?

Asagai (*a sophisticate*). Canadian.

Beneatha (*looking at him*). Asagai, I'm very glad you are back.

Asagai (*looking back at her in turn*). Are you really?

Beneatha. Yes—very.

Asagai. Why?—you were quite glad when I went away. What happened?

Beneatha. You went away.

Asagai. Ahhhhhhhh.

Beneatha. Before—you wanted to be so serious before there was time.

Asagai. How much time must there be before one knows what one feels?

Beneatha (*stalling this particular conversation. Her hands pressed together, in a deliberately childish gesture*). What did you bring me?

Asagai (*handing her the package*). Open it and see.

Beneatha (*eagerly opening the package and drawing out some records and the colorful robes of a Nigerian woman*). Oh, Asagai! . . . You got them for me! . . . How beautiful . . . and the records too!

(*She lifts out the robes and runs to the mirror with them and holds the drapery up in front of herself.*)

Asagai (*coming to her at the mirror*). I shall have to teach you how to drape it properly. (*He flings the material about her for the moment and stands back to look at her.*) Ah—*Oh-pay-gay-day, oh-gbah-mu-shay.* (*A Yoruba exclamation for admiration*) You wear it well . . . very well . . . mutilated hair and all.

Beneatha (*turning suddenly*). My hair—what's wrong with my hair?

Asagai (*shrugging*). Were you born with it like that?

Beneatha (*reaching up to touch it*). No . . . of course not.

[*She looks back to the mirror, disturbed.*]

Asagai (*smiling*). How then?

Beneatha. You know perfectly well how . . . as crinkly as yours . . . that's how.

Asagai. And it is ugly to you that way?

Beneatha (*quickly*). Oh, no—not ugly . . . (*More slowly, apologetically*) But it's so hard to manage when it's, well—raw.

Asagai. And so to accommodate that—you mutilate it every week?

Beneatha. It's not mutilation!

Asagai (*laughing aloud at her seriousness*). Oh . . . please! I am only teasing you because you are so very serious about these things. (*He stands back from her and folds his arms across his chest as he watches her pulling at her hair and frowning in the mirror.*) Do you remember the first time you met me at school? . . . (*He laughs.*) You came up to me and you said—and I thought you were the most serious little thing I had ever seen—you said: (*He imitates her.*) "Mr. Asagai—I want very much to talk with you. About Africa. You see, Mr. Asagai, I am looking for my *identity!*"

[*He laughs.*]

Beneatha (*turning to him, not laughing*). Yes—

[*Her face is quizzical, profoundly disturbed.*]

Asagai (*still teasing and reaching out and taking her face in his hands and turning her profile to him*). Well . . . it is true that this is not so much a profile of a Hollywood queen as perhaps a queen of the Nile—(*A mock dismissal of the importance of the question*) But what does it matter? Assimilationism is so popular in your country.

Beneatha (*wheeling, passionately, sharply*). I am not an assimilationist!

Asagai (*The protest hangs in the room for a moment and* ASAGAI *studies her, his laughter fading.*). Such a serious one. (*There is a pause.*) So—you like the robes? You must take excellent care of them—they are from my sister's personal wardrobe.

Beneatha (*with incredulity*). You—you sent all the way home—for me?

Asagai (*with charm*). For you—I would do much more . . . Well, that is what I came for. I must go.

Beneatha. Will you call me Monday?

Asagai. Yes . . . We have a great deal to talk about. I mean about identity and time and all that.

Beneatha. Time?

Asagai. Yes. About how much time one needs to know what one feels.

Beneatha. You see! You never understood that there is more than one kind of feeling which can exist between a man and a woman—or, at least, there should be.

Asagai (*shaking his head negatively but gently*). No. Between a man and a woman there need be only one kind of feeling. I have that for you . . . Now even . . . right this moment . . .

Beneatha. I know—and by itself—it won't do. I can find that anywhere.

Asagai. For a woman it should be enough.

Beneatha. I know—because that's what it says in all the novels that men write. But it isn't. Go ahead and laugh—but I'm not interested in being someone's little episode in America or—(*with feminine vengeance*)—one of them! (ASAGAI *has burst into laughter again.*) That's funny . . . , huh!

Asagai. It's just that every American girl I have known has said that to me. White—black—in this you are all the same. And the same speech, too!

Beneatha (*angrily*). Yuk, yuk, yuk!

Asagai. It's how you can be sure that the world's most liberated women are not liberated at all. You all talk about it too much!

[MAMA *enters and is immediately all social charm because of the presence of a guest.*]

Beneatha. Oh—Mama—this is Mr. Asagai.

Mama. How do you do?

Asagai (*total politeness to an elder*). How do you do, Mrs. Younger. Please forgive me for coming at such an outrageous hour on a Saturday.

Mama. Well, you are quite welcome. I just hope you understand that our house don't always look like this. (*Chatterish*) You must come again. I would love to hear all about—(*not sure of the name*)—your country. I think it's so sad the way our American Negroes don't know nothing about Africa 'cept Tarzan and all that. And all that money they pour into these churches when they ought to be helping you people over there drive out them French and Englishmen done taken away your land.

[*The mother flashes a slightly superior look at her daughter upon completion of the recitation.*]

Asagai (*taken aback by this sudden and acutely unrelated expression of sympathy*). Yes . . . yes . . .

Mama (*smiling at him suddenly and relaxing and looking him over*). How many miles is it from here to where you come from?

Asagai. Many thousands.

Mama (*looking at him as she would* WALTER). I bet you don't half look after yourself, being away from your mama either. I spec you better come 'round here from time to time to get yourself some decent home-cooked meals . . .

Asagai (*moved*). Thank you. Thank you very much. (*They are all quiet, then*—) Well . . . I must go. I will call you Monday, Alaiyo.

Mama. What's that he call you?

Asagai. Oh—"Alaiyo." I hope you don't mind. It is what you would call a nickname, I think. It is a Yoruba word. I am a Yoruba.

Mama (*looking at* BENEATHA). I—I thought he was from—(*Uncertain*)

Asagai (*understanding*). Nigeria is my country. Yoruba is my tribal origin—

Beneatha. You didn't tell us what Alaiyo means . . . for all I know, you might be calling me Little Idiot or something . . .

Asagai. Well . . . let me see . . . I do not know how just to explain it . . . The sense of a thing can be so different when it changes languages.

Beneatha. You're evading.

Asagai. No—really it is difficult . . . (*Thinking*) It means . . . it means One for Whom Bread—Food—Is Not Enough. (*He looks at her.*) Is that all right?

Beneatha (*understanding, softly*). Thank you.

Mama (*looking from one to the other and not understanding any of it*). Well . . . that's nice . . . You must come see us again—Mr. ——

Asagai. Ah-sah-guy . . .

Mama. Yes . . . Do come again.

Asagai. Goodbye.

[*He exits.*]

Mama (*after him*). Lord, that's a pretty thing just went out here! (*Insinuatingly, to her daughter*) Yes, I guess I see why we done commence to get so interested in Africa 'round here. Missionaries my aunt Jenny!

[*She exits.*]

Beneatha. Oh, Mama! . . .

[*She picks up the Nigerian dress and holds it up to her in front of the mirror again. She sets the headdress on haphazardly and then notices her hair again and clutches at it and then replaces the headdress and frowns at herself. Then she starts to wriggle in front of the mirror as she thinks a Nigerian woman might.* TRAVIS *enters and stands regarding her.*]

Travis. What's the matter, girl, you cracking up?
Beneatha. Shut up.

[*She pulls the headdress off and looks at herself in the mirror and clutches at her hair again and squinches her eyes as if trying to imagine something. Then, suddenly, she gets her raincoat and kerchief and hurriedly prepares for going out.*]

Mama (*coming back into the room*). She's resting now. Travis, baby, run next door and ask Miss Johnson to please let me have a little kitchen cleanser. This here can is empty as Jacob's kettle.
Travis. I just came in.
Mama. Do as you told. (*He exits and she looks at her daughter.*) Where you going?
Beneatha (*halting at the door*). To become a queen of the Nile!

[*She exits in a breathless blaze of glory.* RUTH *appears in the bedroom doorway.*]

Mama. Who told you to get up?
Ruth. Ain't nothing wrong with me to be lying in no bed for. Where did Bennie go?
Mama (*drumming her fingers*). Far as I could make out—to Egypt. (RUTH *just looks at her.*) What time is it getting to?
Ruth. Ten-twenty. And the mailman going to ring that bell this morning just like he done every morning for the last umpteen years.

[TRAVIS *comes in with the cleanser can.*]

Travis. She say to tell you that she don't have much.
Mama (*angrily*). Lord, some people I could name sure is tight-fisted! (*Directing her grandson*) Mark two cans of cleanser down on the list there. If she that hard up for kitchen cleanser, I sure don't want to forget to get her none!
Ruth. Lena—maybe the woman is just short on cleanser—
Mama (*not listening*). —Much baking powder as she done borrowed from me all these years, she could of done gone into the baking business!

[*The bell sounds suddenly and sharply and all three are stunned—*

serious and silent—mid-speech. In spite of all the other conversations and distractions of the morning, this is what they have been waiting for, even TRAVIS, who looks helplessly from his mother to his grandmother. RUTH is the first to come to life again.]

Ruth (to TRAVIS). Get down them steps, boy!

[TRAVIS snaps to life and flies out to get the mail.]

Mama (her eyes wide, her hand to her breast). You mean it done really come?

Ruth (excited). Oh, Miss Lena!

Mama (collecting herself). Well . . . I don't know what we all so excited about 'round here for. We known it was coming for months.

Ruth. That's a whole lot different from having it come and being able to hold it in your hands . . . a piece of paper worth ten thousand dollars . . . (TRAVIS bursts back into the room. He holds the envelope high above his head, like a little dancer, his face is radiant, and he is breathless. He moves to his grandmother with sudden slow ceremony and puts the envelope into her hands. She accepts it, and then merely holds it and looks at it.) Come on! Open it . . . Lord have mercy, I wish Walter Lee was here!

Travis. Open it, Grandmama!

Mama (staring at it). Now you all be quiet. It's just a check.

Ruth. Open it . . .

Mama (still staring at it). Now don't act silly . . . We ain't never been no people to act silly 'bout no money—

Ruth (swiftly). We ain't never had none before—OPEN IT!

[MAMA finally makes a good strong tear and pulls out the thin blue slice of paper and inspects it closely. The boy and his mother study it raptly over MAMA's shoulders.]

Mama. Travis! (She is counting off with doubt.) Is that the right number of zeros.

Travis. Yes'm . . . ten thousand dollars. Gaalee, Grandmama, you rich.

Mama (She holds the check away from her, still looking at it. Slowly her face sobers into a mask of unhappiness.). Ten thousand dollars.

(*She hands it to* RUTH.) Put it away somewhere, Ruth. (*She does not look at* RUTH; *her eyes seem to be seeing something somewhere very far off.*) Ten thousand dollars they give you. Ten thousand dollars.

Travis (*to his mother, sincerely*). What's the matter with Grandmama—don't she want to be rich?

Ruth (*distractedly*). You go on out and play now, baby. (TRAVIS *exits.* MAMA *starts wiping dishes absently, humming intently to herself.* RUTH *turns to her, with kind exasperation.*) You've gone and got yourself upset.

Mama (*not looking at her*). I spec if it wasn't for you all . . . I would just put that money away or give it to the church or something.

Ruth. Now what kind of talk is that. Mr. Younger would just be plain mad if he could hear you talking foolish like that.

Mama (*stopping and staring off*). Yes . . . he sure would. (*Sighing*) We got enough to do with that money, all right. (*She halts then, and turns and looks at her daughter-in-law hard;* RUTH *avoids her eyes and* MAMA *wipes her hands with finality and starts to speak firmly to* RUTH.) Where did you go today, girl?

Ruth. To the doctor.

Mama (*impatiently*). Now, Ruth . . . you know better than that. Old Doctor Jones is strange enough in his way but there ain't nothing 'bout him make somebody slip and call him "she"—like you done this morning.

Ruth. Well, that's what happened—my tongue slipped.

Mama. You went to see that woman, didn't you?

Ruth (*defensively, giving herself away*). What woman you talking about?

Mama (*angrily*). That woman who—

[WALTER *enters in great excitement.*]

Walter. Did it come?

Mama (*quietly*). Can't you give people a Christian greeting before you start asking about money?

Walter (*to* RUTH). Did it come? (RUTH *unfolds the check and lays it quietly before him, watching him intently with thoughts of her own.*

WALTER *sits down and grasps it close and counts off the zeros.*) Ten thousand dollars—(*He turns suddenly, frantically to his mother and draws some papers out of his breast pocket.*) Mama—look. Old Willy Harris put everything on paper—

Mama. Son—I think you ought to talk to your wife . . . I'll go out and leave you alone if you want—

Walter. I can talk to her later—Mama, look—

Mama. Son—

Walter. WILL SOMEBODY PLEASE LISTEN TO ME TODAY!

Mama (*quietly*). I don't 'low no yellin' in this house, Walter Lee, and you know it—(WALTER *stares at them in frustration and starts to speak several times.*) And there ain't going to be no investing in no liquor stores.

Walter. But, Mama, you ain't even looked at it.

Mama. I don't aim to have to speak on that again.

[*A long pause*]

Walter. You ain't looked at it and you don't aim to have to speak on that again? You ain't even looked at it and *you* have decided—(*Crumpling his papers*) Well, *you* tell that to my boy tonight when you put him to sleep on the living-room couch . . . (*Turning to* MAMA *and speaking directly to her*) Yeah—and tell it to my wife, Mama, tomorrow when she has to go out of here to look after somebody else's kids. And tell it to *me,* Mama, every time we need a new pair of curtains and I have to watch *you* go out and work in somebody's kitchen. Yeah, you tell me then!

[WALTER *starts out.*]

Ruth. Where you going?

Walter. I'm going out!

Ruth. Where?

Walter. Just out of this house somewhere—

Ruth (*getting her coat*). I'll come too.

Walter. I don't want you to come!

Ruth. I got something to talk to you about, Walter.

Walter. That's too bad.

Mama (*still quietly*). Walter Lee—(*She waits and he finally turns and looks at her.*) Sit down.

Walter. I'm a grown man, Mama.

Mama. Ain't nobody said you wasn't grown. But you still in my house and my presence. And as long as you are—you'll talk to your wife civil. Now sit down.

Ruth (*suddenly*). Oh, let him go on out and drink himself to death! He makes me sick to my stomach! (*She flings her coat against him and exits to bedroom.*)

Walter (*violently flinging the coat after her*). And you turn mine too, baby! (*The door slams behind her.*) That was my biggest mistake—

Mama (*still quietly*). Walter, what is the matter with you?

Walter. Matter with me? Ain't nothing the matter with *me*!

Mama. Yes there is. Something eating you up like a crazy man. Something more than me not giving you this money. The past few years I been watching it happen to you. You get all nervous acting and kind of wild in the eyes—(WALTER *jumps up impatiently at her words.*) I said sit there now, I'm talking to you!

Walter. Mama—I don't need no nagging at me today.

Mama. Seem like you getting to a place where you always tied up in some kind of knot about something. But if anybody ask you 'bout it you just yell at 'em and bust out the house and go out and drink somewheres. Walter Lee, people can't live with that. Ruth's a good, patient girl in her way—but you getting to be too much. Boy, don't make the mistake of driving that girl away from you.

Walter. Why—what she do for me?

Mama. She loves you.

Walter. Mama—I'm going out. I want to go off somewhere and be by myself for a while.

Mama. I'm sorry 'bout your liquor store, son. It just wasn't the thing for us to do. That's what I want to tell you about—

Walter. I got to go out, Mama—

[*He rises.*]

Mama. It's dangerous, son.

Walter. What's dangerous?

Mama. When a man goes outside his home to look for peace.

Walter (*beseechingly*). Then why can't there never be no peace in this house then?

Mama. You done found it in some other house?

Walter. No—there ain't no woman! Why do women always think there's a woman somewhere when a man gets restless. (*Picks up the check*) Do you know what this money means to me? Do you know what this money can do for us? (*Puts it back*) Mama—Mama—I want so many things . . .

Mama. Yes, son—

Walter. I want so many things that they are driving me kind of crazy . . . Mama—look at me.

Mama. I'm looking at you. You a good-looking boy. You got a job, a nice wife, a fine boy, and—

Walter. A job. (*Looks at her*) Mama, a job? I open and close car doors all day long. I drive a man around in his limousine and I say, "Yes, sir; no, sir; very good, sir; shall I take the Drive, sir?" Mama, that ain't no kind of job . . . that ain't nothing at all. (*Very quietly*) Mama, I don't know if I can make you understand.

Mama. Understand what, baby?

Walter (*quietly*). Sometimes it's like I can see the future stretched out in front of me—just plain as day. The future, Mama. Hanging over there at the edge of my days. Just waiting for me—a big, looming blank space—full of *nothing*. Just waiting for *me*. But it don't have to be. (*Pause. Kneeling beside her chair*) Mama—sometimes when I'm downtown and I pass them cool, quiet-looking restaurants where them white boys are sitting back and talking 'bout things . . . sitting there turning deals worth millions of dollars . . . sometimes I see guys don't look much older than me—

Mama. Son—how come you talk so much 'bout money?

Walter (*with immense passion*). Because it is life, Mama!

Mama (*quietly*). Oh—(*Very quietly*) So now it's life. Money is life. Once upon a time freedom used to be life—now it's money. I guess the world really do change . . .

Walter. No—it was always money, Mama. We just didn't know about it.

Mama. No . . . something has changed. (*She looks at him.*) You something new, boy. In my time we was worried about not being lynched and getting to the North if we could and how to stay alive and still have a pinch of dignity too . . . Now here come you and Beneatha—talking 'bout things we ain't never even thought about hardly, me and your daddy. You ain't satisfied or proud of nothing we done. I mean that you had a home; that we kept you out of trouble till you was grown; that you don't have to ride to work on the back of nobody's streetcar— You my children—but how different we done become.

Walter (*a long beat. He pats her hand and gets up.*). You just don't understand, Mama, you just don't understand.

Mama. Son—do you know your wife is expecting another baby? (WALTER *stands, stunned, and absorbs what his mother has said.*) That's what she wanted to talk to you about. (WALTER *sinks down into a chair.*) This ain't for me to be telling—but you ought to know. (*She waits.*) I think Ruth is thinking 'bout doing something to that child.

Walter (*slowly understanding*). —No—no—Ruth wouldn't do that.

Mama. When the world gets ugly enough—a woman will do anything for her family. *The part that's already living.*

Walter. You don't know Ruth, Mama, if you think she would do that.

[RUTH *opens the bedroom door and stands there a little limp.*]

Ruth (*beaten*). Yes I would too, Walter. (*Pause*) . . .

[*There is total silence as the man stares at his wife and the mother stares at her son.*]

Mama (*presently*). Well— (*Tightly*) Well—son, I'm waiting to hear you say something . . . (*She waits.*) I'm waiting to hear how you be your father's son. Be the man he was . . . (*Pause. The silence shouts.*) Your wife say she going to destroy your child. And I'm waiting to hear you talk like him and say we a people who give children life, not who destroys them—(*She rises.*) I'm waiting to see you stand up and look like your daddy and say we done give up one baby to poverty and that we ain't going to give up nary another one . . . I'm waiting.

Walter. Ruth—(*He can say nothing.*)

Mama. If you a son of mine, tell her! (WALTER *picks up his keys and his coat and walks out. She continues, bitterly.*) You . . . you are a disgrace to your father's memory. Somebody get me my hat!

Curtain

Act Two

Scene 1

Time: Later the same day.

At rise: RUTH *is ironing again. She has the radio going. Presently* BENEATHA'*s bedroom door opens and* RUTH'*s mouth falls and she puts down the iron in fascination.*

Ruth. What have we got on tonight!

Beneatha (*emerging grandly from the doorway so that we can see her thoroughly robed in the costume Asagai brought*). You are looking at what a well-dressed Nigerian woman wears—(*She parades for* RUTH, *her hair completely hidden by the headdress; she is coquettishly fanning herself with an ornate oriental fan, mistakenly more like Butterfly than any Nigerian that ever was.*) Isn't it beautiful? (*She promenades to the radio and, with an arrogant flourish, turns off the good loud blues that is playing.*) Enough of this assimilationist junk! (RUTH *follows her with her eyes as she goes to the phonograph and puts on a record and turns and waits ceremoniously for the music to come up. Then, with a shout—*) OCOMOGOSIAY!

[RUTH *jumps. The music comes up, a lovely Nigerian melody.* BENEATHA *listens, enraptured, her eyes far away—"back to the past." She begins to dance.* RUTH *is dumbfounded.*]

Ruth. What kind of dance is that?
Beneatha. A folk dance.
Ruth (*Pearl Bailey*). What kind of folks do that, honey?
Beneatha. It's from Nigeria. It's a dance of welcome.
Ruth. Who you welcoming?
Beneatha. The men back to the village.
Ruth. Where they been?
Beneatha. How should I know—out hunting or something. Anyway, they are coming back now . . .

Ruth. Well, that's good.

Beneatha (*with the record*).

Alundi, alundi
Alundi alunya
Jop pu a jeepua
Ang gu soooooooooo

Ai yai yae . . .
Ayehaye—alundi . . .

[WALTER *comes in during this performance; he has obviously been drinking. He leans against the door heavily and watches his sister, at first with distaste. Then his eyes look off—"back to the past"—as he lifts both his fists to the roof, screaming.*]

Walter. YEAH . . . AND ETHIOPIA STRETCH FORTH HER HANDS AGAIN! . . .

Ruth (*drily, looking at him*). Yes—and Africa sure is claiming her own tonight. (*She gives them both up and starts ironing again.*)

Walter (*all in a drunken, dramatic shout*). Shut up! . . . I'm digging them drums . . . them drums move me! . . . (*He makes his weaving way to his wife's face and leans in close to her.*) In my *heart of hearts*—(*He thumps his chest.*)—I am much warrior!

Ruth (*without even looking up*). In your heart of hearts you are much drunkard.

Walter (*coming away from her and starting to wander around the room, shouting*). Me and Jomo . . . (*Intently, in his sister's face. She has stopped dancing to watch him in this unknown mood.*) That's my man, Kenyatta. (*Shouting and thumping his chest*) FLAMING SPEAR! . . . (*He is suddenly in possession of an imaginary spear and actively spearing enemies all over the room.*) OCOMOGOSIAY . . .

Beneatha (*to encourage* WALTER, *thoroughly caught up with this side of him*). OCOMOGOSIAY, FLAMING SPEAR!

Walter. THE LION IS WAKING . . . OWIMOWEH! (*He pulls his shirt open and leaps up on the table and gestures with his spear.*)

Beneatha. OWIMOWEH!

Walter (*on the table, very far gone, his eyes pure glass sheets. He sees what we cannot, that he is a leader of his people, a great chief, a descendant of Chaka, and that the hour to march has come.*). Listen,

my black brothers—
Beneatha. OCOMOGOSIAY!
Walter. —Do you hear the waters rushing against the shores of
the coastlands—
Beneatha. OCOMOGOSIAY!
Walter. —Do you hear the screeching of the cocks in yonder
hills beyond where the chiefs meet in council for the coming of
the mighty war—
Beneatha. OCOMOGOSIAY!

[*And now the lighting shifts subtly to suggest the world of* WALTER's
imagination, and the mood shifts from pure comedy. It is the inner
WALTER *speaking; the South Side chauffeur has assumed an un-
expected majesty.*]

Walter. —Do you hear the beating of the wings of the birds fly-
ing low over the mountains and the low places of our land—
Beneatha. OCOMOGOSIAY!
Walter. —Do you hear the singing of the women, singing the
war songs of our fathers to the babies in the great houses?
Singing the sweet war songs! (*The doorbell rings.*) OH, DO YOU
HEAR, MY *BLACK* BROTHERS!
Beneatha (*completely gone*). We hear you, Flaming Spear—

[RUTH *shuts off the phonograph and opens the door.* GEORGE
MURCHISON *enters.*]

Walter. Telling us to prepare for the GREATNESS OF THE
TIME! (*Lights back to normal. He turns and sees* GEORGE.) Black
Brother!

[*He extends his hand for the fraternal clasp.*]

George. Black Brother, . . .
Ruth (*having had enough, and embarrassed for the family*).
Beneatha, you got company—what's the matter with you?
Walter Lee Younger, get down off that table and stop acting like
a fool . . .

[WALTER *comes down off the table suddenly and makes a quick exit to
the bathroom.*]

Ruth. He's had a little to drink . . . I don't know what her excuse is.

George (*to* BENEATHA). Look honey, we're going *to* the theater—we're not going to be *in* it . . . so go change, huh?

[BENEATHA *looks at him and slowly, ceremoniously, lifts her hands and pulls off the headdress. Her hair is close-cropped and unstraightened.* GEORGE *freezes mid-sentence and* RUTH's *eyes all but fall out of her head.*]

George. What in the name of—

Ruth (*touching* BENEATHA's *hair*). Girl, you done lost your natural mind!? Look at your head!

George. What have you done to your head—I mean your hair!

Beneatha. Nothing—except cut it off.

Ruth. Now that's the truth—it's what ain't been done to it! You expect this boy to go out with you with your head all nappy like that?

Beneatha (*looking at* GEORGE). That's up to George. If he's ashamed of his heritage—

George. Oh, don't be so proud of yourself, Bennie—just because you look eccentric.

Beneatha. How can something that's natural be eccentric?

George. That's what being eccentric means—being natural. Get dressed.

Beneatha. I don't like that, George.

Ruth. Why must you and your brother make an argument out of everything people say?

Beneatha. Because I hate assimilationist Negroes!

Ruth. Will somebody please tell me what assimila-whoever means!

George. Oh, it's just a college girl's way of calling people Uncle Toms—but that isn't what it means at all.

Ruth. Well, what does it mean?

Beneatha (*cutting* GEORGE *off and staring at him as she replies to* RUTH). It means someone who is willing to give up his own culture and submerge himself completely in the dominant, and in this case *oppressive* culture!

George. Oh, dear, dear, dear! Here we go! A lecture on the African past! On our Great West African Heritage! In one second we will hear all about the great Ashanti empires; the great Songhay civilizations; and the great sculpture of Benin—and then some poetry in the Bantu—and the whole monologue will end with the word *heritage!* (*Nastily*) Let's face it, baby, your heritage is nothing but a bunch of raggedy . . . spirituals and some grass huts!

Beneatha. GRASS HUTS! (RUTH *crosses to her and forcibly pushes her toward the bedroom.*) See there . . . you are standing there in your splendid ignorance talking about people who were the first to smelt iron on the face of the earth! (RUTH *is pushing her through the door.*) The Ashanti were performing surgical operations when the English—(RUTH *pulls the door to, with* BENEATHA *on the other side, and smiles graciously at* GEORGE. BENEATHA *opens the door and shouts the end of the sentence defiantly at* GEORGE.)—were still tattooing themselves with blue dragons! (*She goes back inside.*)

Ruth. Have a seat, George. (*They both sit.* RUTH *folds her hands rather primly on her lap, determined to demonstrate the civilization of the family.*) Warm, ain't it? I mean for September. (*Pause*) Just like they always say about Chicago weather: If it's too hot or cold for you, just wait a minute and it'll change. (*She smiles happily at this cliché of clichés.*) Everybody say it's got to do with them bombs and things they keep setting off. (*Pause*) Would you like a nice cold beer?

George. No, thank you. I don't care for beer. (*He looks at his watch.*) I hope she hurries up.

Ruth. What time is the show?

George. It's an eight-thirty curtain. That's just Chicago, though. In New York standard curtain time is eight-forty.

[*He is rather proud of this knowledge.*]

Ruth (*properly appreciating it*). You get to New York a lot?

George (*offhand*). Few times a year.

Ruth. Oh—that's nice. I've never been to New York.

[WALTER *enters. We feel he has relieved himself, but the edge of unreality is still with him.*]

Walter. New York ain't got nothing Chicago ain't. Just a bunch of hustling people all squeezed up together—being "Eastern."

[*He turns his face into a screw of displeasure.*]

George. Oh—you've been?

Walter. *Plenty* of times.

Ruth (*shocked at the lie*). Walter Lee Younger!

Walter (*staring her down*). Plenty! (*Pause*) What we got to drink in this house? Why don't you offer this man some refreshment. (*To* GEORGE) They don't know how to entertain people in this house, man.

George. Thank you—I don't really care for anything.

Walter (*feeling his head; sobriety coming*). Where's Mama?

Ruth. She ain't come back yet.

Walter (*looking* MURCHISON *over from head to toe, scrutinizing his carefully casual tweed sports jacket over cashmere V-neck sweater over soft eyelet shirt and tie, and soft slacks, finished off with white buckskin shoes*). Why all you college boys wear them funny-looking white shoes?

Ruth. Walter Lee!

[GEORGE MURCHISON *ignores the remark.*]

Walter (*to* RUTH). Well, they look crazy . . . white shoes, cold as it is.

Ruth (*crushed*). You have to excuse him—

Walter. No he don't! Excuse me for what? What you always excusing me for! I'll excuse myself when I needs to be excused! (*A pause*) They look as funny as them black knee socks Beneatha wears out of here all the time.

Ruth. It's the college *style*, Walter.

Walter. Style?! She looks like she got burnt legs or something!

Ruth. Oh, Walter—

Walter (*an irritable mimic*). Oh, Walter! Oh, Walter! (*To* MUR-CHISON) How's your old man making out? I understand you all going to buy that big hotel on the Drive? (*He finds a beer in the refrigerator, wanders over to* MURCHISON, *sipping and wiping his lips with the back of his hand, and straddling a chair backwards to talk to* *the other man.*) Shrewd move. Your old man is all right, man. (*Tapping his head and half winking for emphasis*) I mean he knows how to operate. I mean he thinks *big*, you know what I mean, I mean for a *home*, you know? But I think he's kind of running out of ideas now. I'd like to talk to him. Listen, man, I got some plans that could turn this city upside down. I mean think like he does. *Big.* Invest big, gamble big, shoot, lose *big* if you have to, you know what I mean. It's hard to find a man on this whole South Side who understands my kind of thinking—you dig? (*He scrutinizes* MURCHISON *again, drinks his beer, squints his eyes, and leans in close, confidential, man to man.*) Me and you ought to sit down and talk sometimes, man. Man, I got me some ideas . . .

Murchison (*with boredom*). Yeah—sometimes we'll have to do that, Walter.

Walter (*understanding the indifference, and offended*). Yeah—well, when you get the time, man. I know you a busy little boy.

Ruth. Walter, please—

Walter (*bitterly, hurt*). I know ain't nothing in this world as busy as you colored college boys with your fraternity pins and white shoes . . .

Ruth (*covering her face with humiliation*). Oh, Walter Lee—

Walter. I see you all all the time—with the books tucked under your arms—going to your (*British A—a mimic*) "clahsses." And for what! What in the world you learning over there? Filling up your heads—(*counting off on his fingers*)—with the sociology and the psychology—but they teaching you how to be a man? How to take over and run the world? They teaching you how to run a rubber plantation or a steel mill? Naw—just to talk proper and read books and wear them funny-looking white shoes . . .

George (*looking at him with distaste, a little above it all*). You're all wacked up with bitterness, man.

Walter (*intently, almost quietly, between the teeth, glaring at the boy*). And you—ain't you bitter, man? Ain't you just about had it yet? Don't you see no stars gleaming that you can't reach out and grab? You happy?—You contented turkey—you happy? You got it made? Bitter? Man, I'm a volcano. Bitter? Here I am a giant—surrounded by ants! Ants who can't even understand what it is the giant is talking about.

Ruth (*passionately and suddenly*). Oh, Walter—ain't you with nobody!

Walter (*violently*). No! 'Cause ain't nobody with me! Not even my own mother!

Ruth. Walter, that's a terrible thing to say!

[BENEATHA *enters, dressed for the evening in a cocktail dress and earrings, hair natural.*]

George. Well—hey—(*Crosses to* BENEATHA; *thoughtful, with emphasis, since this is a reversal*) You look great!

Walter (*seeing his sister's hair for the first time*). What's the matter with your head?

Beneatha (*tired of the jokes now*). I cut it off, Brother.

Walter (*coming close to inspect it and walking around her*). Well, I'll be damned. So that's what they mean by the African bush . . .

Beneatha. Ha ha. Let's go, George.

George (*looking at her*). You know something? I like it. It's sharp. I mean it really is. (*Helps her into her wrap*)

Ruth. Yes—I think so, too. (*She goes to the mirror and starts to clutch at her hair.*)

Walter. Oh no! You leave yours alone, baby. You might turn out to have a pin-shaped head or something!

Beneatha. See you all later.

Ruth. Have a nice time.

George. Thanks. Good night. (*Half out the door, he reopens it. To* WALTER) Good night, Prometheus!

[BENEATHA *and* GEORGE *exit.*]

Walter (*to* RUTH). Who is Prometheus?

Ruth. I don't know. Don't worry about it.

Walter (*in fury, pointing after* GEORGE). See there—they get to a point where they can't insult you man to man—they got to go talk about something ain't nobody never heard of!

Ruth. How do you know it was an insult? (*To humor him*) Maybe Prometheus is a nice fellow.

Walter. Prometheus! I bet there ain't even no such thing! I bet that simple-minded clown—
Ruth. Walter—

[*She stops what she is doing and looks at him.*]

Walter (*yelling*). Don't start!
Ruth. Start what?
Walter. Your nagging! Where was I? Who was I with? How much money did I spend?
Ruth (*plaintively*). Walter Lee—why don't we just try to talk about it . . .
Walter (*not listening*). I been out talking with people who understand me. People who care about the things I got on my mind.
Ruth (*wearily*). I guess that means people like Willy Harris.
Walter. Yes, people like Willy Harris.
Ruth (*with a sudden flash of impatience*). Why don't you all just hurry up and go into the banking business and stop talking about it!
Walter. Why? You want to know why? 'Cause we all tied up in a race of people that don't know how to do nothing but moan, pray, and have babies!

[*The line is too bitter even for him and he looks at her and sits down.*]

Ruth. Oh, Walter . . . (*Softly*) Honey, why can't you stop fighting me?
Walter (*without thinking*). Who's fighting you? Who even cares about you?

[*This line begins the retardation of his mood.*]

Ruth. Well—(*She waits a long time, and then with resignation starts to put away her things.*) I guess I might as well go on to bed . . . (*More or less to herself*) I don't know where we lost it . . . but we have . . . (*Then, to him*) I—I'm sorry about this new baby, Walter. I guess maybe I better go on and do what I started . . . I guess I just didn't realize how bad things was with us . . . I guess I just didn't really realize—(*She starts out to the bedroom and stops.*) You want some hot milk?

Walter. Hot milk?

Ruth. Yes—hot milk.

Walter. Why hot milk?

Ruth. 'Cause after all that liquor you come home with you ought to have something hot in your stomach.

Walter. I don't want no milk.

Ruth. You want some coffee then?

Walter. No, I don't want no coffee. I don't want nothing hot to drink. (*Almost plaintively*) Why you always trying to give me something to eat?

Ruth (*standing and looking at him helplessly*). What *else* can I give you, Walter Lee Younger?

[*She stands and looks at him and presently turns to go out again. He lifts his head and watches her going away from him in a new mood which began to emerge when he asked her "Who cares about you?"*]

Walter. It's been rough, ain't it, baby? (*She hears and stops but does not turn around and he continues to her back.*) I guess between two people there ain't never as much understood as folks generally thinks there is. I mean like between me and you—(*She turns to face him.*) How we gets to the place where we scared to talk softness to each other. (*He waits, thinking hard himself.*) Why you think it got to be like that? (*He is thoughtful, almost as a child would be.*) Ruth, what is it gets into people ought to be close?

Ruth. I don't know, honey. I think about it a lot.

Walter. On account of you and me, you mean? The way things are with us. The way something done come down between us.

Ruth. There ain't so much between us, Walter . . . Not when you come to me and try to talk to me. Try to be with me . . . a little even.

Walter (*total honesty*). Sometimes . . . sometimes . . . I don't even know how to try.

Ruth. Walter—

Walter. Yes?

Ruth (*coming to him, gently and with misgiving, but coming to him*). Honey . . . life don't have to be like this. I mean sometimes people can do things so that things are better . . . You remember how we used to talk when Travis was born . . . about the way we were going to live . . . the kind of house . . . (*She is stroking his head.*) Well, it's all starting to slip away from us . . .

[*He turns her to him and they look at each other and kiss, tenderly and hungrily. The door opens and* MAMA *enters—*WALTER *breaks away and jumps up. A beat*]

Walter. Mama, where have you been?
Mama. My—them steps is longer than they used to be. Whew! (*She sits down and ignores him.*) How you feeling this evening, Ruth?

[RUTH *shrugs, disturbed at having been interrupted and watching her husband knowingly.*]

Walter. Mama, where have you been all day?
Mama (*still ignoring him and leaning on the table and changing to more comfortable shoes*). Where's Travis?
Ruth. I let him go out earlier and he ain't come back yet. Boy, is he going to get it!
Walter. Mama!
Mama (*as if she has heard him for the first time*). Yes, son?
Walter. Where did you go this afternoon?
Mama. I went downtown to tend to some business that I had to tend to.
Walter. What kind of business?
Mama. You know better than to question me like a child, Brother.
Walter (*rising and bending over the table*). Where were you, Mama? (*Bringing his fists down and shouting*) Mama, you didn't do something with that insurance money, something crazy?

[*The front door opens slowly, interrupting him, and* TRAVIS *peeks his head in, less than hopefully.*]

Travis (*to his mother*). Mama, I—
Ruth. "Mama I" nothing! You're going to get it, boy! Get on in that bedroom and get yourself ready!

Travis. But I—
Mama. Why don't you all never let the child explain hisself.
Ruth. Keep out of it now, Lena.

[MAMA *clamps her lips together, and* RUTH *advances toward her son menacingly.*]

Ruth. A thousand times I have told you not to go off like that—
Mama (*holding out her arms to her grandson*). Well—at least let me tell him something. I want him to be the first one to hear . . . Come here, Travis. (*The boy obeys, gladly.*) Travis—(*She takes him by the shoulder and looks into his face.*)—you know that money we got in the mail this morning?
Travis. Yes'm—
Mama. Well—what you think your grandmama gone and done with that money?
Travis. I don't know, Grandmama.
Mama (*putting her finger on his nose for emphasis*). She went out and she bought you a house! (*The explosion comes from* WALTER *at the end of the revelation and he jumps up and turns away from all of them in a fury.* MAMA *continues, to* TRAVIS.) You glad about the house? It's going to be yours when you get to be a man.
Travis. Yeah—I always wanted to live in a house.
Mama. All right, gimme some sugar then—(TRAVIS *puts his arms around her neck as she watches her son over the boy's shoulder. Then, to* TRAVIS, *after the embrace*) Now when you say your prayers tonight, you thank God and your grandfather—'cause it was him who give you the house—in his way.
Ruth (*taking the boy from* MAMA *and pushing him toward the bedroom*). Now you get out of here and get ready for your beating.
Travis. Aw, Mama—
Ruth. Get on in there—(*Closing the door behind him and turning radiantly to her mother-in-law*) So you went and did it!
Mama (*quietly, looking at her son with pain*). Yes, I did.
Ruth (*raising both arms classically*). PRAISE GOD! (*Looks at* WALTER *a moment, who says nothing. She crosses rapidly to her husband.*) Please, honey—let me be glad . . . you be glad too. (*She has laid*

her hands on his shoulders, but he shakes himself free of her roughly, without turning to face her.) Oh, Walter . . . a home . . . *a home. (She comes back to* MAMA.) Well—where is it? How big is it? How much it going to cost?

Mama. Well—

Ruth. When we moving?

Mama (*smiling at her*). First of the month.

Ruth (*throwing back her head with jubilance*). *Praise God!*

Mama (*tentatively, still looking at her son's back turned against her and* RUTH). It's—it's a nice house too . . . (*She cannot help speaking directly to him. An imploring quality in her voice, her manner, makes her almost like a girl now.*) Three bedrooms—nice big one for you and Ruth. . . . Me and Beneatha still have to share our room, but Travis have one of his own—and (*with difficulty*) I figure if the—new baby—is a boy, we could get one of them double-decker outfits . . . And there's a yard with a little patch of dirt where I could maybe get to grow me a few flowers . . . And a nice big basement . . .

Ruth. Walter honey, be glad—

Mama (*still to his back, fingering things on the table*). 'Course I don't want to make it sound fancier than it is . . . It's just a plain little old house—but it's made good and solid—and it will be *ours*. Walter Lee—it makes a difference in a man when he can walk on floors that belong to *him* . . .

Ruth. Where is it?

Mama (*frightened at this telling*). Well—well—it's out there in Clybourne Park—

[RUTH's *radiance fades abruptly, and* WALTER *finally turns slowly to face his mother with incredulity and hostility.*]

Ruth. Where?

Mama (*matter-of-factly*). Four o six Clybourne Street, Clybourne Park.

Ruth. Clybourne Park? Mama, there ain't no colored people living in Clybourne Park.

Mama (*almost idiotically*). Well, I guess there's going to be some now.

Walter (*bitterly*). So that's the peace and comfort you went out and bought for us today!

Mama (*raising her eyes to meet his finally*). Son—I just tried to find the nicest place for the least amount of money for my family.

Ruth (*trying to recover from the shock*). Well—well—'course I ain't one never been 'fraid of no crackers, mind you—but—well, wasn't there no other houses nowhere?

Mama. Them houses they put up for colored in them areas way out all seem to cost twice as much as other houses. I did the best I could.

Ruth (*Struck senseless with the news, in its various degrees of goodness and trouble, she sits a moment, her fists propping her chin in thought, and then she starts to rise, bringing her fists down with vigor, the radiance spreading from cheek to cheek again.*). Well—well!—All I can say is—if this is my time in life—MY TIME—to say goodbye—(*and she builds with momentum as she starts to circle the room with an exuberant, almost tearfully happy release.*)—to these . . . cracking walls!—(*She pounds the walls.*)—and these marching roaches!—(*She wipes at an imaginary army of marching roaches.*)—and this cramped little closet which ain't now or never was no kitchen! . . . then I say it loud and good, HAL-LELUJAH! AND GOODBYE MISERY . . . I DON'T NEVER WANT TO SEE YOUR UGLY FACE AGAIN! (*She laughs joyously, having practically destroyed the apartment, and flings her arms up and lets them come down happily, slowly, reflectively, over her abdomen, aware for the first time perhaps that the life therein pulses with happiness and not despair.*) Lena?

Mama (*moved, watching her happiness*). Yes, honey?

Ruth (*looking off*). Is there—is there a whole lot of sunlight?

Mama (*understanding*). Yes, child, there's a whole lot of sunlight.

[*Long pause*]

Ruth (*collecting herself and going to the door of the room* TRAVIS *is in*). Well—I guess I better see 'bout Travis. (*To* MAMA) Lord, I sure don't feel like whipping nobody today!

[*She exits.*]

Mama (*The mother and son are left alone now and the mother waits a long time, considering deeply, before she speaks.*). Son—you—you understand what I done, don't you? (WALTER *is silent and sullen.*) I—I just seen my family falling apart today . . . just falling to pieces in front of my eyes . . . We couldn't of gone on like we was today. We was going backwards 'stead of forwards—talking 'bout not wanting babies and wishing each other was dead . . . When it gets like that in life—you just got to do something different, push on out and do something bigger . . . (*She waits.*) I wish you say something, son . . . I wish you'd say how deep inside you you think I done the right thing—

Walter (*crossing slowly to his bedroom door and finally turning there and speaking measuredly*). What you need me to say you done right for? *You* the head of this family. You run our lives like you want to. It was your money and you did what you wanted with it. So what you need for me to say it was all right for? (*Bitterly, to hurt her as deeply as he knows is possible*) So you butchered up a dream of mine—you—who always talking 'bout your children's dreams . . .

Mama. Walter Lee—

[*He just closes the door behind him.* MAMA *sits alone, thinking heavily.*]

Curtain

Scene 2

Time: Friday night. A few weeks later.
At rise: Packing crates mark the intention of the family to move.
BENEATHA *and* GEORGE *come in, presumably from an evening out again.*

George. O.K. . . . O.K., whatever you say . . . (*They both sit on the couch. He tries to kiss her. She moves away.*) Look, we've had a nice evening; let's not spoil it, huh? . . .

[*He again turns her head and tries to nuzzle in and she turns away from him, not with distaste but with momentary lack of interest; in a mood to pursue what they were talking about.*]

Beneatha. I'm *trying* to talk to you.
George. We always talk.
Beneatha. Yes—and I love to talk.
George (*exasperated; rising*). I know it and I don't mind it some-times . . . I want you to cut it out, see—The moody stuff, I mean. I don't like it. You're a nice-looking girl . . . all over. That's all you need, honey, forget the atmosphere. Guys aren't going to go for the atmosphere—they're going to go for what they see. Be glad for that. Drop the Garbo routine. It doesn't go with you. As for myself, I want a nice—(*groping*)—simple (*thoughtfully*)—sophisticated girl . . . not a poet—O.K.?

[*He starts to kiss her, she rebuffs him again, and he jumps up.*]

Beneatha. Why are you angry, George?
George. Because this is stupid! I don't go out with you to discuss the nature of "quiet desperation" or to hear all about your thoughts—because the world will go on thinking what it thinks regardless—
Beneatha. Then why read books? Why go to school?
George (*with artificial patience, counting on his fingers*). It's simple. You read books—to learn facts—to get grades—to pass the course—to get a degree. That's all—it has nothing to do with thoughts.

[*A long pause*]

Beneatha. I see. (*He starts to sit.*) Good night, George.

[GEORGE *looks at her a little oddly, and starts to exit. He meets* MAMA *coming in.*]

George. Oh—hello, Mrs. Younger.

Mama. Hello, George, how you feeling?

George. Fine—fine, how are you?

Mama. Oh, a little tired. You know them steps can get you after a day's work. You all have a nice time tonight?

George. Yes—a fine time. A fine time.

Mama. Well, good night.

George. Good night. (*He exits.* MAMA *closes the door behind her.*)

Mama. Hello, honey. What you sitting like that for?

Beneatha. I'm just sitting.

Mama. Didn't you have a nice time?

Beneatha. No.

Mama. No? What's the matter?

Beneatha. Mama, George is a fool—honest. (*She rises.*)

Mama (*hustling around unloading the packages she has entered with. She stops.*). Is he, baby?

Beneatha. Yes.

[BENEATHA *makes up* TRAVIS's *bed as she talks.*]

Mama. You sure?

Beneatha. Yes.

Mama. Well—I guess you better not waste your time with no fools.

[BENEATHA *looks up at her mother, watching her put groceries in the refrigerator. Finally she gathers up her things and starts into the bedroom. At the door she stops and looks back at her mother.*]

Beneatha. Mama—

Mama. Yes, baby—

Beneatha. Thank you.

Mama. For what?

Beneatha. For understanding me this time.

[*She exits quickly and the mother stands, smiling a little, looking at the place where* BENEATHA *just stood.* RUTH *enters.*]

Ruth. Now don't you fool with any of this stuff, Lena—
Mama. Oh, I just thought I'd sort a few things out. Is Brother here?
Ruth. Yes.
Mama (*with concern*). Is he—
Ruth (*reading her eyes*). Yes.

[MAMA *is silent and someone knocks on the door.* MAMA *and* RUTH *exchange weary and knowing glances and* RUTH *opens it to admit the neighbor,* MRS. JOHNSON, *who is a rather squeaky wide-eyed lady of no particular age, with a newspaper under her arm.*]

Mama (*changing her expression to acute delight and a ringing cheerful greeting*). Oh—hello there, Johnson.
Johnson (*This is a woman who decided long ago to be enthusiastic about EVERYTHING in life and she is inclined to wave her wrist vigorously at the height of her exclamatory comments.*). Hello there, yourself! H'you this evening, Ruth?
Ruth (*not much of a deceptive type*). Fine, Mis' Johnson, h'you?
Johnson. Fine. (*Reaching out quickly, playfully, and patting* RUTH's *stomach*) Ain't you starting to poke out none yet! (*She mugs with delight at the overfamiliar remark and her eyes dart around looking at the crates and packing preparation;* MAMA's *face is a cold sheet of endurance.*) Oh, ain't we getting ready round here, though! Yessir! Lookathere! I'm telling you the Youngers is really getting ready to "move on up a little higher!"—Bless God!
Mama (*a little drily, doubting the total sincerity of the Blesser*). Bless God.
Johnson. He's good, ain't He?
Mama. Oh yes, He's good.
Johnson. I mean sometimes He works in mysterious ways . . . but He works, don't He!
Mama (*the same*). Yes, He does.
Johnson. I'm just soooooo happy for y'all. And this here

child—(*about* RUTH) looks like she could just pop open with happiness, don't she. Where's all the rest of the family?

Mama. Bennie's gone to bed—

Johnson. Ain't no . . . (*The implication is pregnancy.*) sickness done hit you—I hope . . . ?

Mama. No—she just tired. She was out this evening.

Johnson (*All is a coo, an emphatic coo.*). Aw—ain't that lovely. She still going out with the little Murchison boy?

Mama (*drily*). Ummmm huh.

Johnson. That's lovely. You sure got lovely children, Younger. Me and Isaiah talks all the time 'bout what fine children you was blessed with. We sure do.

Mama. Ruth, give Mis' Johnson a piece of sweet potato pie and some milk.

Johnson. Oh honey, I can't stay hardly a minute—I just dropped in to see if there was anything I could do. (*Accepting the food easily*) I guess y'all seen the news what's all over the colored paper this week . . .

Mama. No—didn't get mine yet this week.

Johnson (*lifting her head and blinking with the spirit of catastrophe*). You mean you ain't read 'bout them colored people that was bombed out their place out there?

[RUTH *straightens with concern and takes the paper and reads it.* JOHNSON *notices her and feeds commentary.*]

Johnson. Ain't it something how bad these here white folks is getting here in Chicago! Lord, getting so you think you right down in Mississippi! (*With a tremendous and rather insincere sense of melodrama*) 'Course I thinks it's wonderful how our folks keeps on pushing out. You hear some of those Negroes round here talking 'bout how they don't go where they ain't wanted and all that—but not me, honey! (*This is a lie.*) Wilhemenia Othella Johnson goes anywhere, any time she feels like it! (*With head movement for emphasis*) Yes I do! Why if we left it up to these here crackers, the poor niggers wouldn't have nothing—(*She clasps her hand over her mouth.*) Oh, I always forgets you don't 'low that word in your house.

Mama (*quietly, looking at her*). No—I don't 'low it.

Johnson (*vigorously again*). Me neither! I was just telling Isaiah yesterday when he come using it in front of me—I said, "Isaiah, it's just like Mis' Younger says all the time—"

Mama. Don't you want some more pie?

Johnson. No—no thank you; this was lovely. I got to get on over home and have my midnight coffee. I hear some people say it don't let them sleep but I finds I can't close my eyes right lessen I done had that laaaast cup of coffee . . . (*She waits. A beat. Undaunted*) My Good-night coffee, I calls it!

Mama (*with much eye-rolling and communication between herself and* RUTH). Ruth, why don't you give Mis' Johnson some coffee.

[RUTH *gives* MAMA *an unpleasant look for her kindness.*]

Johnson (*accepting the coffee*). Where's Brother tonight?

Mama. He's lying down.

Johnson. MMmmmmm, he sure gets his beauty rest, don't he? Good-looking man. Sure is a good-looking man! (*Reaching out to pat* RUTH'*s stomach again*) I guess that's how come we keep on having babies around here. (*She winks at* MAMA.) One thing 'bout Brother, he always know how to have a *good* time. And soooooo ambitious! I bet it was his idea y'all moving out to Clybourne Park. Lord—I bet this time next month y'all's names will have been in the papers plenty—(*Holding up her hands to mark off each word of the headline she can see in front of her*) "NEGROES INVADE CLYBOURNE PARK—BOMBED!"

Mama (*She and* RUTH *look at the woman in amazement.*). We ain't exactly moving out there to get bombed.

Johnson. Oh, honey—you know I'm praying to God every day that don't nothing like that happen! But you have to think of life like it is—and these here Chicago peckerwoods is some baaaad peckerwoods.

Mama (*wearily*). We done thought about all that Mis' Johnson.

[BENEATHA *comes out of the bedroom in her robe and passes through to the bathroom.* MRS. JOHNSON *turns.*]

Johnson. Hello there, Bennie!

Beneatha (*crisply*). Hello, Mrs. Johnson.

Johnson. How is school?

Beneatha (*crisply*). Fine, thank you. (*She goes out.*)

Johnson (*insulted*). Getting so she don't have much to say to nobody.

Mama. The child was on her way to the bathroom.

Johnson. I know—but sometimes she act like ain't got time to pass the time of day with nobody ain't been to college. Oh—I ain't criticizing her none. It's just—you know how some of our young people gets when they get a little education. (MAMA *and* RUTH *say nothing, just look at her.*) Yes—well. Well, I guess I better get on home. (*Unmoving*) 'Course I can understand how she must be proud and everything—being the only one in the family to make something of herself. I know just being a chauffeur ain't never satisfied Brother none. He shouldn't feel like that, though. Ain't nothing wrong with being a chauffeur.

Mama. There's plenty wrong with it.

Johnson. What?

Mama. Plenty. My husband always said being any kind of servant wasn't a fit thing for a man to have to be. He always said a man's hands was made to make things, or to turn the earth with—not to drive nobody's car for 'em—or—(*She looks at her own hands.*) carry they slop jars. And my boy is just like him—he wasn't meant to wait on nobody.

Johnson (*rising, somewhat offended*). Mmmmmmmmm. The Youngers is too much for me! (*She looks around.*) You sure one proud-acting bunch of colored folks. Well—I always thinks like Booker T. Washington said that time—"Education has spoiled many a good plow hand"—

Mama. Is that what old Booker T. said?

Johnson. He sure did.

Mama. Well, it sounds just like him. The fool.

Johnson (*indignantly*). Well—he was one of our great men.

Mama. Who said so?

Johnson (*nonplussed*). You know, me and you ain't never agreed about some things, Lena Younger. I guess I better be going—

Ruth (*quickly*). Good night.
Johnson. Good night. Oh—(*Thrusting it at her*) You can keep the paper! (*With a trill*) 'Night.
Mama. Good night, Mis' Johnson.

[MRS. JOHNSON *exits.*]

Ruth. If ignorance was gold . . .
Mama. Shush. Don't talk about folks behind their backs.
Ruth. You do.
Mama. I'm old and corrupted. (BENEATHA *enters.*) You was rude to Mis' Johnson, Beneatha, and I don't like it at all.
Beneatha (*at her door*). Mama, if there are two things we, as a people, have got to overcome, one is the Ku Klux Klan—and the other is Mrs. Johnson. (*She exits.*)
Mama. Smart aleck.

[*The phone rings.*]

Ruth. I'll get it.
Mama. Lord, ain't this a popular place tonight.
Ruth (*at the phone*). Hello—Just a minute. (*Goes to door*) Walter, it's Mrs. Arnold. (*Waits. Goes back to the phone. Tense*) Hello. Yes, this is his wife speaking . . . He's lying down now. Yes . . . well, he'll be in tomorrow. He's been very sick. Yes—I know we should have called, but we were so sure he'd be able to come in today. Yes—yes, I'm very sorry. Yes . . . Thank you very much. (*She hangs up.* WALTER *is standing in the doorway of the bedroom behind her.*) That was Mrs. Arnold.
Walter (*indifferently*). Was it?
Ruth. She said if you don't come in tomorrow that they are getting a new man . . .
Walter. Ain't that sad—ain't that crying sad.
Ruth. She said Mr. Arnold has had to take a cab for three days . . . Walter, you ain't been to work for three days! (*This is a revelation to her.*) Where you been, Walter Lee Younger? (WALTER *looks at her and starts to laugh.*) You're going to lose your job.
Walter. That's right . . . (*He turns on the radio.*)

Ruth. Oh, Walter, and with your mother working like a dog every day—

[*A steamy, deep blues pours into the room.*]

Walter. That's sad too— Everything is sad.

Mama. What you been doing for these three days, son?

Walter. Mama—you don't know all the things a man what got leisure can find to do in this city . . . What's this—Friday night? Well—Wednesday I borrowed Willy Harris's car and I went for a drive . . . just me and myself and I drove and drove . . . Way out . . . way past South Chicago, and I parked the car and I sat and looked at the steel mills all day long. I just sat in the car and looked at them big black chimneys for hours. Then I drove back and I went to the Green Hat. (*Pause*) And Thursday— Thursday I borrowed the car again and I got in it and I pointed it the other way and I drove the other way—for hours—way, way up to Wisconsin, and I looked at the farms. I just drove and looked at the farms. Then I drove back and I went to the Green Hat. (*Pause*) And today—today I didn't get the car. Today I just walked. All over the South Side. And I looked at the Negroes and they looked at me and finally I just sat down on the curb at Thirty-ninth and South Parkway and I just sat there and watched the Negroes go by. And then I went to the Green Hat. You all sad? You all depressed? And you know where I am going right now—

[RUTH *goes out quietly.*]

Mama. Oh, Big Walter, is this the harvest of our days?

Walter. You know what I like about the Green Hat? I like this little cat they got there who blows a sax . . . He blows. He talks to me. He ain't but 'bout five feet tall and he's got a conked head and his eyes is always closed and he's all music—

Mama (*rising and getting some papers out of her handbag*). Walter—

Walter. And there's this other guy who plays the piano . . . and they got a sound. I mean they can work on some music . . . They got the best little combo in the world in the Green Hat . . . You can just sit there and drink and listen to them three men play and you realize that don't nothing matter in this whole world, but just being there—

Mama. I've helped do it to you, haven't I, son? Walter I been wrong.

Walter. Naw—you ain't never been wrong about nothing, Mama.

Mama. Listen to me, now. I say I been wrong, son. That I been doing to you what the rest of the world been doing to you. (*She turns off the radio.*) Walter—(*She stops and he looks up slowly at her and she meets his eyes pleadingly.*) What you ain't never understood is that I ain't got nothing, don't own nothing, ain't never really wanted nothing that wasn't for you. There ain't nothing as precious to me . . . There ain't nothing worth holding on to, money, dreams, nothing else—if it means—if it means it's going to destroy my boy. (*She takes an envelope out of her handbag and puts it in front of him and he watches her without speaking or moving.*) I paid the man thirty-five hundred dollars down on the house. That leaves sixty-five hundred dollars. Monday morning I want you to take this money and take three thousand dollars and put it in a savings account for Beneatha's medical schooling. The rest you put in a checking account— with your name on it. And from now on any penny that come out of it or that go in it is for you to look after. For you to decide. (*She drops her hands a little helplessly.*) It ain't much, but it's all I got in the world and I'm putting it in your hands. I'm telling you to be the head of this family from now on like you supposed to be.

Walter (*stares at the money*). You trust me like that, Mama?

Mama. I ain't never stop trusting you. Like I ain't never stop loving you.

[*She goes out, and* WALTER *sits looking at the money on the table. Finally, in a decisive gesture, he gets up, and, in mingled joy and desperation, picks up the money. At the same moment,* TRAVIS *enters for bed.*]

Travis. What's the matter, Daddy? You drunk?

Walter (*sweetly, more sweetly than we have ever known him*). No, Daddy ain't drunk. Daddy ain't going to never be drunk again. . . .

Travis. Well, good night, Daddy.

[*The* FATHER *has come from behind the couch and leans over, embracing his son.*]

Walter. Son, I feel like talking to you tonight.

Travis. About what?

Walter. Oh, about a lot of things. About you and what kind of man you going to be when you grow up. . . . Son—son, what do you want to be when you grow up?

Travis. A bus driver.

Walter (*laughing a little*). A what? Man, that ain't nothing to want to be!

Travis. Why not?

Walter. 'Cause, man—it ain't big enough—you know what I mean.

Travis. I don't know then. I can't make up my mind. Sometimes Mama asks me that too. And sometimes when I tell her I just want to be like you—she says she don't want me to be like that and sometimes she says she does. . . .

Walter (*gathering him up in his arms*). You know what, Travis? In seven years you going to be seventeen years old. And things is going to be very different with us in seven years, Travis. . . . One day when you are seventeen I'll come home—home from my office downtown somewhere—

Travis. You don't work in no office, Daddy.

Walter. No—but after tonight. After what your daddy gonna do tonight, there's going to be offices—a whole lot of offices. . . .

Travis. What you gonna do tonight, Daddy?

Walter. You wouldn't understand yet, son, but your daddy's gonna make a transaction . . . a business transaction that's going to change our lives. . . . That's how come one day when you 'bout seventeen years old I'll come home and I'll be pretty tired, you know what I mean, after a day of conferences and secretaries getting things wrong the way they do . . . 'cause an executive's life is hard, man—(*The more he talks the farther away he gets.*) And I'll pull the car up on the driveway . . . just a plain black Chrysler, I think, with white walls—no—black tires. More elegant. Rich people don't have to be flashy . . . though I'll have to get something a little sportier for Ruth—maybe a Cadillac convertible to do her shopping in. . . . And I'll come up the steps to the house and the gardener will be clipping away at the hedges and he'll say, "Good evening, Mr. Younger." And I'll say, "Hello, Jefferson, how are you this evening?" And I'll go inside and Ruth will come downstairs and meet me at the door and we'll kiss each other and she'll take my arm and we'll go up to your room to see you sitting on the floor with the catalogues of all the great schools in America around you. . . . All the great schools in the world! And—and I'll say, all right son— it's your seventeenth birthday, what is it you've decided? . . . Just tell me where you want to go to school and you'll *go.* Just tell me, what it is you want to be—and you'll *be* it. . . . Whatever you want to be—Yessir! (*He holds his arms open for* TRAVIS.) You just name it, son . . . (TRAVIS *leaps into them.*) and I hand you the world!

[WALTER's *voice has risen in pitch and hysterical promise and on the last line he lifts* TRAVIS *high.*]

Blackout

Scene 3

Time: Saturday, moving day, one week later.
Before the curtain rises, RUTH's *voice, a strident, dramatic church alto, cuts through the silence.*

It is, in the darkness, a triumphant surge, a penetrating statement of expectation: "Oh, Lord, I don't feel no ways tired! Children, oh, glory hallelujah!"

As the curtain rises we see that RUTH *is alone in the living room, finishing up the family's packing. It is moving day. She is nailing crates and tying cartons.* BENEATHA *enters, carrying a guitar case, and watches her exuberant sister-in-law.*

Ruth. Hey!

Beneatha (*putting away the case*). Hi.

Ruth (*pointing at a package*). Honey—look in that package there and see what I found on sale this morning at the South Center. (RUTH *gets up and moves to the package and draws out some curtains.*) Lookahere—hand-turned hems!

Beneatha. How do you know the window size out there?

Ruth (*who hadn't thought of that*). Oh—Well, they bound to fit something in the whole house. Anyhow, they was too good a bargain to pass up. (RUTH *slaps her head, suddenly remembering something.*) Oh, Bennie—I meant to put a special note on that carton over there. That's your mama's good china and she wants 'em to be very careful with it.

Beneatha. I'll do it.

[BENEATHA *finds a piece of paper and starts to draw large letters on it.*]

Ruth. You know what I'm going to do soon as I get in that new house?

Beneatha. What?

Ruth. Honey—I'm going to run me a tub of water up to here . . . (*With her fingers practically up to her nostrils*) And I'm going to get in it—and I am going to sit . . . and sit . . . and sit in that hot water and the first person who knocks to tell *me* to hurry up and come out—

Beneatha. Gets shot at sunrise.

Ruth (*laughing happily*). You said it, sister! (*Noticing how large* BENEATHA *is absent-mindedly making the note*) Honey, they ain't going to read that from no airplane.

Beneatha (*laughing herself*). I guess I always think things have more emphasis if they are big, somehow.

Ruth (*looking up at her and smiling*). You and your brother seem to have that as a philosophy of life. Lord, that man—done changed so 'round here. You know—you know what we did last night? Me and Walter Lee?

Beneatha. What?

Ruth (*smiling to herself*). We went to the movies. (*Looking at* BENEATHA *to see if she understands*) We went to the movies. You know the last time me and Walter went to the movies together?

Beneatha. No.

Ruth. Me neither. That's how long it been. (*Smiling again*) But we went last night. The picture wasn't much good, but that didn't seem to matter. We went—and we held hands.

Beneatha. Oh, Lord!

Ruth. We held hands—and you know what?

Beneatha. What?

Ruth. When we come out of the show it was late and dark and all the stores and things was closed up . . . and it was kind of chilly and there wasn't many people on the streets . . . and we was still holding hands, me and Walter.

Beneatha. You're killing me.

[WALTER *enters with a large package. His happiness is deep in him; he cannot keep still with his newfound exuberance. He is singing and wiggling and snapping his fingers. He puts his package in a corner and puts a phonograph record, which he has brought in with him, on the record player. As the music, soulful and sensuous, comes up he dances over to* RUTH *and tries to get her to dance with him. She gives in at last to his raunchiness and in a fit of giggling allows herself to be drawn into his mood. They dip and she melts into his arms in a classic, body-melding "slow drag."*]

Beneatha (*regarding them a long time as they dance, then drawing* *in her breath for a deeply exaggerated comment which she does not particularly mean).* Talk about—oldddddddddddfash-ionedddddddd—Negroes!

Walter *(stopping momentarily).* What kind of Negroes?

[*He says this in fun. He is not angry with her today, nor with anyone. He starts to dance with his wife again.*]

Beneatha. Old-fashioned.

Walter *(as he dances with* RUTH*).* You know, when these *New Negroes* have their convention—(*pointing at his sister*)—that is going to be the chairman of the Committee on Unending Agitation. (*He goes on dancing, then stops.*) Race, race, race! . . . Girl, I do believe you are the first person in the history of the entire human race to successfully brainwash yourself. (BENEATHA *breaks up and he goes on dancing. He stops again, enjoying his tease.*) Shoot, even the N double A C P takes a holiday sometimes! (BENEATHA *and* RUTH *laugh. He dances with* RUTH *some more and starts to laugh and stops and pantomimes someone over an operating table.*) I can just see that chick someday looking down at some poor cat on an operating table and before she starts to slice him, she says . . . (*Pulling his sleeves back maliciously*) "By the way, what are your views on civil rights down there? . . ."

[*He laughs at her again and starts to dance happily. The bell sounds.*]

Beneatha. Sticks and stones may break my bones but . . . words will never hurt me!

[BENEATHA *goes to the door and opens it as* WALTER *and* RUTH *go on with the clowning.* BENEATHA *is somewhat surprised to see a quiet-looking middle-aged white man in a business suit holding his hat and a briefcase in his hand and consulting a small piece of paper.*]

Man. Uh—how do you do, miss. I am looking for a Mrs.—(*He looks at the slip of paper.*) Mrs. Lena Younger? (*He stops short, struck dumb at the sight of the oblivious* WALTER *and* RUTH.)

Beneatha *(smoothing her hair with slight embarrassment).* Oh—yes, that's my mother. Excuse me. (*She closes the door and turns to quiet the other two.*) Ruth! Brother! (*Enunciating precisely but* *soundlessly: "There's a white man at the door!" They stop dancing,* RUTH *cuts off the phonograph,* BENEATHA *opens the door. The man casts a curious quick glance at all of them.)* Uh—come in please.

Man (*coming in*). Thank you.

Beneatha. My mother isn't here just now. Is it business?

Man. Yes . . . well, of a sort.

Walter (*freely, the Man of the House*). Have a seat. I'm Mrs. Younger's son. I look after most of her business matters.

[RUTH *and* BENEATHA *exchange amused glances.*]

Man (*regarding* WALTER, *and sitting*). Well—My name is Karl Lindner . . .

Walter (*stretching out his hand*). Walter Younger. This is my wife—(RUTH *nods politely.*)—and my sister.

Lindner. How do you do.

Walter (*amiably, as he sits himself easily on a chair, leaning forward on his knees with interest and looking expectantly into the newcomer's face*). What can we do for you, Mr. Lindner!

Lindner (*some minor shuffling of the hat and briefcase on his knees*). Well—I am a representative of the Clybourne Park Improvement Association—

Walter (*pointing*). Why don't you sit your things on the floor?

Lindner. Oh—yes. Thank you. (*He slides the briefcase and hat under the chair.*) And as I was saying—I am from the Clybourne Park Improvement Association and we have had it brought to our attention at the last meeting that you people—or at least your mother—has bought a piece of residential property at—(*He digs for the slip of paper again.*)—four o six Clybourne Street . . .

Walter. That's right. Care for something to drink? Ruth, get Mr. Lindner a beer.

Lindner (*upset for some reason*). Oh—no, really. I mean thank you very much, but no thank you.

Ruth (*innocently*). Some coffee?

Lindner. Thank you, nothing at all.

[BENEATHA *is watching the man carefully.*]

Lindner. Well, I don't know how much you folks know about our organization. (*He is a gentle man; thoughtful and somewhat labored in his manner.*) It is one of these community organizations set up to look after—oh, you know, things like block upkeep and special projects and we also have what we call our New Neighbors Orientation Committee . . .

Beneatha (*drily*). Yes—and what do they do?

Lindner (*turning a little to her and then returning the main force to* WALTER). Well—it's what you might call a sort of welcoming committee, I guess. I mean they, we—I'm the chairman of the committee—go around and see the new people who move into the neighborhood and sort of give them the lowdown on the way we do things out in Clybourne Park.

Beneatha (*with appreciation of the two meanings, which escape* RUTH *and* WALTER). Un-huh.

Lindner. And we also have the category of what the association calls—(*He looks elsewhere.*)—uh—special community problems . . .

Beneatha. Yes—and what are some of those?

Walter. Girl, let the man talk.

Lindner (*with understated relief*). Thank you. I would sort of like to explain this thing in my own way. I mean I want to explain to you in a certain way.

Walter. Go ahead.

Lindner. Yes. Well. I'm going to try to get right to the point. I'm sure we'll all appreciate that in the long run.

Beneatha. Yes.

Walter. Be still now!

Lindner. Well—

Ruth (*still innocently*). Would you like another chair—you don't look comfortable.

Lindner (*more frustrated than annoyed*). No, thank you very much. Please. Well—to get right to the point I—(*A great breath, and he is off at last.*) I am sure you people must be aware of some of the incidents which have happened in various parts of the city when colored people have moved into certain areas—(BENEATHA *exhales heavily and starts tossing a piece of fruit up and down in the air.*) Well—because we have what I think is going to

be a unique type of organization in American community life—
not only do we deplore that kind of thing—but we are trying to
do something about it. (BENEATHA *stops tossing and turns with a
new and quizzical interest to the man.*) We feel—(*gaining confi-
dence in his mission because of the interest in the faces of the people he
is talking to*)—we feel that most of the trouble in this world,
when you come right down to it—(*He hits his knee for emphasis.*)—most of the trouble exists because people just don't sit
down and talk to each other.

Ruth (*nodding as she might in church, pleased with the remark*). You
can say that again, mister.

Lindner (*more encouraged by such affirmation*). That we don't try
hard enough in this world to understand the other fellow's
problem. The other guy's point of view.

Ruth. Now that's right.

[BENEATHA *and* WALTER *merely watch and listen with genuine
interest.*]

Lindner. Yes—that's the way we feel out in Clybourne Park.
And that's why I was elected to come here this afternoon and
talk to you people. Friendly like, you know, the way people
should talk to each other and see if we couldn't find some way
to work this thing out. As I say, the whole business is a matter of
caring about the other fellow. Anybody can see that you are a
nice family of folks, hard working and honest I'm sure.
(BENEATHA *frowns slightly, quizzically, her head tilted regarding him.*)
Today everybody knows what it means to be on the outside of
something. And of course, there is always somebody who is out
to take advantage of people who don't always understand.

Walter. What do you mean?

Lindner. Well—you see our community is made up of people
who've worked hard as the dickens for years to build up that
little community. They're not rich and fancy people; just hard-
working, honest people who don't really have much but those
little homes and a dream of the kind of community they want
to raise their children in. Now, I don't say we are perfect and
there is a lot wrong in some of the things they want. But you've

got to admit that a man, right or wrong, has the right to want to have the neighborhood he lives in a certain kind of way. And at the moment the overwhelming majority of our people out there feel that people get along better, take more of a common interest in the life of the community, when they share a common background. I want you to believe me when I tell you that race prejudice simply doesn't enter into it. It is a matter of the people of Clybourne Park believing, rightly or wrongly, as I say, that for the happiness of all concerned that our Negro families are happier when they live in their *own* communities.

Beneatha (*with a grand and bitter gesture*). This, friends, is the Welcoming Committee!

Walter (*dumbfounded, looking at* LINDNER). Is this what you came marching all the way over here to tell us?

Lindner. Well, now we've been having a fine conversation. I hope you'll hear me all the way through.

Walter (*tightly*). Go ahead, man.

Lindner. You see—in the face of all the things I have said, we are prepared to make your family a very generous offer . . .

Beneatha. Thirty pieces and not a coin less!

Walter. Yeah?

Lindner (*putting on his glasses and drawing a form out of the briefcase*). Our association is prepared, through the collective effort of our people, to buy the house from you at a financial gain to your family.

Ruth. Lord have mercy, ain't this the living gall!

Walter. All right, you through?

Lindner. Well, I want to give you the exact terms of the financial arrangement—

Walter. We don't want to hear no exact terms of no arrangements. I want to know if you got any more to tell us 'bout getting together?

Lindner (*taking off his glasses*). Well—I don't suppose that you feel . . .

Walter. Never mind how I feel—you got any more to say 'bout how people ought to sit down and talk to each other? . . . Get out of my house, man.

[*He turns his back and walks to the door.*]

Lindner (*looking around at the hostile faces and reaching and assembling his hat and briefcase*). Well—I don't understand why you people are reacting this way. What do you think you are going to gain by moving into a neighborhood where you just aren't wanted and where some elements—well—people can get awful worked up when they feel that their whole way of life and everything they've ever worked for is threatened.

Walter. Get out.

Lindner (*at the door, holding a small card*). Well—I'm sorry it went like this.

Walter. Get out.

Lindner (*almost sadly regarding* WALTER). You just can't force people to change their hearts, son.

[*He turns and puts his card on a table and exits.* WALTER *pushes the door to with stinging hatred, and stands looking at it.* RUTH *just sits and* BENEATHA *just stands. They say nothing.* MAMA *and* TRAVIS *enter.*]

Mama. Well—this all the packing got done since I left out of here this morning. I testify before God that my children got all the energy of the *dead*! What time the moving men due?

Beneatha. Four o'clock. You had a caller, Mama.

[*She is smiling, teasingly.*]

Mama. Sure enough—who?

Beneatha (*her arms folded saucily*). The Welcoming Committee.

[WALTER *and* RUTH *giggle.*]

Mama (*innocently*). Who?

Beneatha. The Welcoming Committee. They said they're sure going to be glad to see you when you get there.

Walter (*devilishly*). Yeah, they said they can't hardly wait to see your face.

[*Laughter*]

Mama (*sensing their facetiousness*). What's the matter with you all?

Walter. Ain't nothing the matter with us. We just telling you 'bout the gentleman who came to see you this afternoon. From the Clybourne Park Improvement Association.

Mama. What he want?

Ruth (*in the same mood as* BENEATHA *and* WALTER). To welcome you, honey.

Walter. He said they can't hardly wait. He said the one thing they don't have, that they just *dying* to have out there is a fine family of fine colored people! (*To* RUTH *and* BENEATHA) Ain't that right!

Ruth (*mockingly*). Yeah! He left his card—

Beneatha (*handing card to* MAMA). In case.

[MAMA *reads and throws it on the floor—understanding and looking off as she draws her chair up to the table on which she has put her plant and some sticks and some cord.*]

Mama. Father, give us strength. (*Knowingly—and without fun*) Did he threaten us?

Beneatha. Oh—Mama—they don't do it like that any more. He talked Brotherhood. He said everybody ought to learn how to sit down and hate each other with good Christian fellowship.

[*She and* WALTER *shake hands to ridicule the remark.*]

Mama (*sadly*). Lord, protect us . . .

Ruth. You should hear the money those folks raised to buy the house from us. All we paid and then some.

Beneatha. What they think we going to do—eat 'em?

Ruth. No, honey, marry 'em.

Mama (*shaking her head*). Lord, Lord, Lord . . .

Ruth. Well—that's the way the crackers crumble. (*A beat*) Joke.

Beneatha (*laughingly noticing what her mother is doing*). Mama, what are you doing?

Mama. Fixing my plant so it won't get hurt none on the way . . .

Beneatha. Mama, you going to take *that* to the new house?

Mama. Un-huh—

Beneatha. That raggedy-looking old thing?

Mama (*stopping and looking at her*). It expresses ME!

Ruth (*with delight, to* BENEATHA). So there, Miss Thing!

[WALTER *comes to* MAMA *suddenly and bends down behind her and squeezes her in his arms with all his strength. She is overwhelmed by the suddenness of it and, though delighted, her manner is like that of* RUTH *and* TRAVIS.]

Mama. Look out now, boy! You make me mess up my thing here!

Walter (*His face lit, he slips down on his knees beside her, his arms still about her.*). Mama . . . you know what it means to climb up in the chariot?

Mama (*gruffly, very happy*). Get on away from me now . . .

Ruth (*near the gift-wrapped package, trying to catch* WALTER's *eye*). Psst—

Walter. What the old song say, Mama . . .

Ruth. Walter—Now?

[*She is pointing at the package.*]

Walter (*speaking the lines, sweetly, playfully, in his mother's face*).
I got wings . . . you got wings . . .
All God's children got wings . . .

Mama. Boy—get out of my face and do some work . . .

Walter.
When I get to heaven gonna put on my wings,
Gonna fly all over God's heaven . . .

Beneatha (*teasingly, from across the room*). Everybody talking 'bout heaven ain't going there!

Walter (*to* RUTH, *who is carrying the box across to them*). I don't know, you think we ought to give her that . . . Seems to me she ain't been very appreciative around here.

Mama (*eyeing the box, which is obviously a gift*). What is that?

Walter (*taking it from* RUTH *and putting it on the table in front of* MAMA). Well—what you all think? Should we give it to her?

Ruth. Oh—she was pretty good today.

Mama. I'll good you—

[*She turns her eyes to the box again.*]

Beneatha. Open it, Mama.

[*She stands up, looks at it, turns and looks at all of them, and presses her hands together and does not open the package.*]

Walter (*sweetly*). Open it, Mama. It's for you. (MAMA *looks in his eyes. It is the first present in her life without its being Christmas. Slowly she opens her package and lifts out, one by one, a brand-new sparkling set of gardening tools.* WALTER *continues, prodding.*) Ruth made up the note—read it . . .

Mama (*picking up the card and adjusting her glasses*). "To our own Mrs. Miniver—Love from Brother, Ruth, and Beneatha." Ain't that lovely . . .

Travis (*tugging at his father's sleeve*). Daddy, can I give her mine now?

Walter. All right, son. (TRAVIS *flies to get his gift.*)

Mama. Now I don't have to use my knives and forks no more . . .

Walter. Travis didn't want to go in with the rest of us, Mama. He got his own. (*Somewhat amused*) We don't know what it is . . .

Travis (*racing back in the room with a large hatbox and putting it in front of his grandmother*). Here!

Mama. Lord have mercy, baby. You done gone and bought your grandmother a hat?

Travis (*very proud*). Open it!

[*She does and lifts out an elaborate, but very elaborate, wide gardening hat, and all the adults break up at the sight of it.*]

Ruth. Travis, honey, what is that?

Travis (*who thinks it is beautiful and appropriate*). It's a gardening hat! Like the ladies always have on in the magazines when they work in their gardens.

Beneatha (*giggling fiercely*). Travis—we were trying to make Mama Mrs. Miniver—not Scarlett O'Hara!

Mama (*indignantly*). What's the matter with you all! This here is a beautiful hat! (*Absurdly*) I always wanted me one just like it!

[*She pops it on her head to prove it to her grandson, and the hat is ludicrous and considerably oversized.*]

Ruth. Hot dog! Go, Mama!

Walter (*doubled over with laughter*). I'm sorry, Mama—but you look like you ready to go out and chop you some cotton sure enough!

[*They all laugh except* MAMA, *out of deference to* TRAVIS'S *feelings.*]

Mama (*gathering the boy up to her*). Bless your heart—this is the prettiest hat I ever owned—(WALTER, RUTH, *and* BENEATHA *chime in—noisily, festively, and insincerely congratulating* TRAVIS *on his gift.*) What are we all standing around here for? We ain't finished packin' yet. Bennie, you ain't packed one book.

[*The bell rings.*]

Beneatha. That couldn't be the movers . . . it's not hardly two good yet—

[BENEATHA *goes into her room.* MAMA *starts for door.*]

Walter (*turning, stiffening*). Wait—wait—I'll get it.

[*He stands and looks at the door.*]

Mama. You expecting company, son?

Walter (*just looking at the door*). Yeah—yeah . . .

[MAMA *looks at* RUTH, *and they exchange innocent and unfrightened glances.*]

Mama (*not understanding*). Well, let them in, son.

Beneatha (*from her room*). We need some more string.

Mama. Travis—you run to the hardware and get me some string cord.

[MAMA *goes out and* WALTER *turns and looks at* RUTH. TRAVIS *goes to a dish for money.*]

Ruth. Why don't you answer the door, man?

Walter (*suddenly bounding across the floor to embrace her*). 'Cause sometimes it hard to let the future begin! (*Stooping down in her face*)

I got wings! You got wings!
All God's children got wings!

(*He crosses to the door and throws it open. Standing there is a very slight little man in a not too prosperous business suit and with haunted frightened eyes and a hat pulled down tightly, brim up, around his forehead.* TRAVIS *passes between the men and exits.* WALTER *leans deep in the man's face, still in his jubilance.*)

When I get to heaven gonna put on my wings,
Gonna fly all over God's heaven . . .

(*The little man just stares at him.*)

Heaven—

(*Suddenly he stops and looks past the little man into the empty hallway.*) Where's Willy, man?

Bobo. He ain't with me.
Walter (*not disturbed*). Oh—come on in. You know my wife.
Bobo (*dumbly, taking off his hat*). Yes—h'you, Miss Ruth.
Ruth (*quietly, a mood apart from her husband already, seeing* BOBO). Hello, Bobo.
Walter. You right on time today . . . Right on time. That's the way! (*He slaps* BOBO *on his back.*) Sit down . . . lemme hear.

[RUTH *stands stiffly and quietly in back of them, as though somehow she senses death, her eyes fixed on her husband.*]

Bobo (*his frightened eyes on the floor, his hat in his hands*). Could I please get a drink of water, before I tell you about it, Walter Lee?

[WALTER *does not take his eyes off the man.* RUTH *goes blindly to the tap and gets a glass of water and brings it to* BOBO.]

Walter. There ain't nothing wrong, is there?
Bobo. Lemme tell you—
Walter. Man—didn't nothing go wrong?

Bobo. Lemme tell you—Walter Lee. (*Looking at* RUTH *and talking to her more than to* WALTER) You know how it was. I got to tell you how it was. I mean first I got to tell you how it was all the way . . . I mean about the money I put in, Walter Lee . . .

Walter (*with taut agitation now*). What about the money you put in?

Bobo. Well—it wasn't much as we told you—me and Willy— (*He stops.*) I'm sorry, Walter. I got a bad feeling about it. I got a real bad feeling about it . . .

Walter. Man, what you telling me about all this for? . . . Tell me what happened in Springfield . . .

Bobo. Springfield.

Ruth (*like a dead woman*). What was supposed to happen in Springfield?

Bobo (*to her*). This deal that me and Walter went into with Willy—Me and Willy was going to go down to Springfield and spread some money 'round so's we wouldn't have to wait so long for the liquor license . . . That's what we were going to do. Everybody said that was the way you had to do, you understand, Miss Ruth?

Walter. Man—what happened down there?

Bobo (*a pitiful man, near tears*). I'm trying to tell you, Walter.

Walter (*screaming at him suddenly*). THEN TELL ME, DAMMIT . . . WHAT'S THE MATTER WITH YOU?

Bobo. Man . . . I didn't go to no Springfield, yesterday.

Walter (*halted, life hanging in the moment*). Why not?

Bobo (*the long way, the hard way to tell*). 'Cause I didn't have no reasons to . . .

Walter. Man, what are you talking about!

Bobo. I'm talking about the fact that when I got to the train station yesterday morning—eight o'clock like we planned . . . Man—*Willy didn't never show up.*

Walter. Why . . . where was he . . . where is he?

Bobo. That's why I'm trying to tell you . . . I don't know . . . I waited six hours . . . I called his house . . . and I waited . . . six hours . . . I waited in that train station six hours . . . (*Breaking into tears*) That was all the extra money I had in the world . . .

(*Looking up at* WALTER *with the tears running down his face*) Man, Willy is gone.

Walter. Gone, what you mean Willy is gone? Gone where? You mean he went by himself. You mean he went off to Springfield by himself—to take care of getting the license—(*Turns and looks anxiously at* RUTH) You mean maybe he didn't want too many people in on the business down there? (*Looks to* RUTH *again, as before*) You know Willy got his own ways. (*Looks back to* BOBO) Maybe you was late yesterday and he just went on down there without you. Maybe—maybe—he's been callin' you at home tryin' to tell you what happened or something. Maybe— maybe—he just got sick. He's somewhere—he's got to be somewhere. We just got to find him—me and you got to find him. (*Grabs* BOBO *senselessly by the collar and starts to shake him*) We got to!

Bobo (*in sudden angry, frightened agony*). What's the matter with you, Walter! *When a cat take off with your money he don't leave you no road maps!*

Walter (*turning madly, as though he is looking for* WILLY *in the very room*). Willy! . . . Willy . . . don't do it . . . Please don't do it . . . Man, not with that money . . . Man, please, not with that money . . . Oh, God . . . Don't let it be true . . . (*He is wandering around, crying out for* WILLY *and looking for him or perhaps for help from God.*) Man . . . I trusted you . . . Man, I put my life in your hands . . . (*He starts to crumple down on the floor as* RUTH *just covers her face in horror.* MAMA *opens the door and comes into the room, with* BENEATHA *behind her.*) Man . . . (*He starts to pound the floor with his fists, sobbing wildly.*) THAT MONEY IS MADE OUT OF MY FATHER'S FLESH——

Bobo (*standing over him helplessly*). I'm sorry, Walter . . . (*Only* WALTER's *sobs reply.* BOBO *puts on his hat.*) I had my life staked on this deal, too . . .

[*He exits.*]

Mama (*to* WALTER). Son—(*She goes to him, bends down to him, talks to his bent head.*) Son . . . Is it gone? Son, I gave you sixty-five hundred dollars. Is it gone? All of it? Beneatha's money too?

Walter (*lifting his head slowly*). Mama . . . I never . . . went to the bank at all . . .

Mama (*not wanting to believe him*). You mean . . . your sister's school money . . . you used that too . . . Walter? . . .

Walter. Yessss! All of it . . . It's all gone . . .

[*There is total silence.* RUTH *stands with her face covered with her hands;* BENEATHA *leans forlornly against a wall, fingering a piece of red ribbon from the mother's gift.* MAMA *stops and looks at her son without recognition and then, quite without thinking about it, starts to beat him senselessly in the face.* BENEATHA *goes to them and stops it.*]

Beneatha. Mama!

[MAMA *stops and looks at both of her children and rises slowly and wanders vaguely, aimlessly away from them.*]

Mama. I seen . . . him . . . night after night . . . come in . . . and look at that rug . . . and then look at me . . . the red showing in his eyes . . . the veins moving in his head . . . I seen him grow thin and old before he was forty . . . working and working and working like somebody's old horse . . . killing himself . . . and you—you give it all away in a day—(*She raises her arms to strike him again.*)

Beneatha. Mama—

Mama. Oh, God . . . (*She looks up to Him.*) Look down here—and show me the strength.

Beneatha. Mama—

Mama (*folding over*). Strength . . .

Beneatha (*plaintively*). Mama . . .

Mama. Strength!

Curtain

Act Three

An hour later.

At curtain, there is a sullen light of gloom in the living room, gray light not unlike that which began the first scene of Act One. At left we can see WALTER *within his room, alone with himself. He is stretched out on the bed, his shirt out and open, his arms under his head. He does not smoke, he does not cry out, he merely lies there, looking up at the ceiling, much as if he were alone in the world.*

In the living room BENEATHA *sits at the table, still surrounded by the now almost ominous packing crates. She sits looking off. We feel that this is a mood struck perhaps an hour before, and it lingers now, full of the empty sound of profound disappointment. We see on a line from her brother's bedroom the sameness of their attitudes. Presently the bell rings and* BENEATHA *rises without ambition or interest in answering. It is* ASAGAI, *smiling broadly, striding into the room with energy and happy expectation and conversation.*

Asagai. I came over . . . I had some free time. I thought I might help with the packing. Ah, I like the look of packing crates! A household in preparation for a journey! It depresses some people . . . but for me . . . it is another feeling. Something full of the flow of life, do you understand? Movement, progress . . . It makes me think of Africa.

Beneatha. Africa!

Asagai. What kind of a mood is this? Have I told you how deeply you move me?

Beneatha. He gave away the money, Asagai . . .

Asagai. Who gave away what money?

Beneatha. The insurance money. My brother gave it away.

Asagai. Gave it away?

Beneatha. He made an investment! With a man even Travis wouldn't have trusted with his most worn-out marbles.

Asagai. And it's gone?

Beneatha. Gone!

Asagai. I'm very sorry . . . And you, now?

Beneatha. Me? . . . Me? . . . Me, I'm nothing . . . Me. When I was very small . . . we used to take our sleds out in the wintertime and the only hills we had were the ice-covered stone steps of some houses down the street. And we used to fill them in with snow and make them smooth and slide down them all day . . . and it was very dangerous, you know . . . far too steep . . . and sure enough one day a kid named Rufus came down too fast and hit the sidewalk and we saw his face just split open right there in front of us . . . And I remember standing there looking at his bloody open face thinking that was the end of Rufus. But the ambulance came and they took him to the hospital and they fixed the broken bones and they sewed it all up . . . and the next time I saw Rufus he just had a little line down the middle of his face . . . I never got over that . . .

Asagai. What?

Beneatha. That that was what one person could do for another, fix him up—sew up the problem, make him all right again. That was the most marvelous thing in the world . . . I wanted to do that. I always thought it was the one concrete thing in the world that a human being could do. Fix up the sick, you know—and make them whole again. This was truly being God . . .

Asagai. You wanted to be God?

Beneatha. No—I wanted to cure. It used to be so important to me. I wanted to cure. It used to matter. I used to care. I mean about people and how their bodies hurt . . .

Asagai. And you've stopped caring?

Beneatha. Yes—I think so.

Asagai. Why?

Beneatha (*bitterly*). Because it doesn't seem deep enough, close enough to what ails mankind! It was a child's way of seeing things—or an idealist's.

Asagai. Children see things very well sometimes—and idealists even better.

Beneatha. I know that's what you think. Because you are still where I left off. You with all your talk and dreams about Africa! You still think you can patch up the world. Cure the Great Sore of Colonialism—(*loftily, mocking it*) with the Penicillin of Independence—!

Asagai. Yes!

Beneatha. Independence *and then what*? What about all the crooks and thieves and just plain idiots who will come into power and steal and plunder the same as before—only now they will be black and do it in the name of the new Independence—WHAT ABOUT THEM?!

Asagai. That will be the problem for another time. First we must get there.

Beneatha. And where does it end?

Asagai. End? Who even spoke of an end? To life? To living?

Beneatha. An end to misery! To stupidity! Don't you see there isn't any real progress, Asagai, there is only one large circle that we march in, around and around, each of us with our own little picture in front of us—our own little mirage that we think is the future.

Asagai. That is the mistake.

Beneatha. What?

Asagai. What you just said—about the circle. It isn't a circle—it is simply a long line—as in geometry, you know, one that reaches into infinity. And because we cannot see the end—we also cannot see how it changes. And it is very odd but those who see the changes—who dream, who will not give up—are called idealists . . . and those who see only the circle—we call *them* the "realists"!

Beneatha. Asagai, while I was sleeping in that bed in there, people went out and took the future right out of my hands! And nobody asked me, nobody consulted me—they just went out and changed my life!

Asagai. Was it your money?

Beneatha. What?

Asagai. Was it your money he gave away?

Beneatha. It belonged to all of us.

Asagai. But did you earn it? Would you have had it at all if your father had not died?

Beneatha. No.

Asagai. Then isn't there something wrong in a house—in a world—where all dreams, good or bad, must depend on the death of a man? I never thought to see *you* like this, Alaiyo. You! Your brother made a mistake and you are grateful to him so that now you can give up the ailing human race on account of it! You talk about what good is struggle, what good is anything! Where are we all going and why are we bothering!

Beneatha. AND YOU CANNOT ANSWER IT!

Asagai (*shouting over her*). *I LIVE THE ANSWER!* (*Pause*) In my village at home it is the exceptional man who can even read a newspaper . . . or who ever sees a book at all. I will go home and much of what I will have to say will seem strange to the people of my village. But I will teach and work and things will happen, slowly and swiftly. At times it will seem that nothing changes at all . . . and then again the sudden dramatic events which make history leap into the future. And then quiet again. Retrogression even. Guns, murder, revolution. And I even will have moments when I wonder if the quiet was not better than all that death and hatred. But I will look about my village at the illiteracy and disease and ignorance and I will not wonder long. And perhaps . . . perhaps I will be a great man . . . I mean perhaps I will hold on to the substance of truth and find my way always with the right course . . . and perhaps for it I will be butchered in my bed some night by the servants of empire . . .

Beneatha. *The martyr!*

Asagai (*He smiles.*). . . . or perhaps I shall live to be a very old man, respected and esteemed in my new nation . . . And perhaps I shall hold office and this is what I'm trying to tell you, Alaiyo: Perhaps the things I believe now for my country will be wrong and outmoded, and I will not understand and do terrible things to have things my way or merely to keep my power. Don't you see that there will be young men and women—not British soldiers then, but my own black countrymen—to step out of the shadows some evening and slit my then useless throat? Don't you see they have always been there . . . that they always will be. And that such a thing as my own death will be an advance? They who might kill me even . . . actually replenish all that I was.

Beneatha. Oh, Asagai, I know all that.

Asagai. Good! Then stop moaning and groaning and tell me what you plan to do.

Beneatha. Do?

Asagai. I have a bit of a suggestion.

Beneatha. What?

Asagai (*rather quietly for him*). That when it is all over—that you come home with me—

Beneatha (*staring at him and crossing away with exasperation*). Oh—Asagai—at this moment you decide to be romantic!

Asagai (*quickly understanding the misunderstanding*). My dear, young creature of the New World—I do not mean across the city—I mean across the ocean: home—to Africa.

Beneatha (*slowly understanding and turning to him with murmured amazement*). To Africa?

Asagai. Yes! . . . (*Smiling and lifting his arms playfully*) Three hundred years later the African Prince rose up out of the seas and swept the maiden back across the middle passage over which her ancestors had come—

Beneatha (*unable to play*). To—to Nigeria?

Asagai. Nigeria. Home. (*Coming to her with genuine romantic flippancy*) I will show you our mountains and our stars; and give you cool drinks from gourds and teach you the old songs and the ways of our people—and, in time, we will pretend that—(*very softly*)—you have only been away for a day. Say that you'll come—(*He swings her around and takes her full in his arms in a kiss which proceeds to passion.*)

Beneatha (*pulling away suddenly*). You're getting me all mixed up—

Asagai. Why?

Beneatha. Too many things—too many things have happened today. I must sit down and think. I don't know what I feel about anything right this minute.

[*She promptly sits down and props her chin on her fist.*]

Asagai (*charmed*). All right, I shall leave you. No—don't get up. (*Touching her, gently, sweetly*) Just sit awhile and think . . . Never be afraid to sit awhile and think. (*He goes to door and looks at her.*) How often I have looked at you and said, "Ah—so this is what the New World hath finally wrought . . ."

[*He exits.* BENEATHA *sits alone. Presently* WALTER *enters from his room and starts to rummage through things, feverishly looking for something. She looks up and turns in her seat.*]

Beneatha (*hissingly*). Yes—just look at what the New World hath wrought! . . . Just look! (*She gestures with bitter disgust.*) There he is! *Monsieur le petit bourgeois noir*—himself! There he is—Symbol of a Rising Class! Entrepreneur! Titan of the system! (WALTER *ignores her completely and continues frantically and destructively looking for something and hurling things to floor and tearing things out of their place in his search.* BENEATHA *ignores the eccentricity of his actions and goes on with the monologue of insult.*) Did you dream of yachts on Lake Michigan, Brother? Did you see yourself on that Great Day sitting down at the Conference Table, surrounded by all the mighty bald-headed men in America? All halted, waiting, breathless, waiting for your pronouncements on industry? Waiting for you—Chairman of the Board! (WALTER *finds what he is looking for—a small piece of white paper—and pushes it in his pocket and puts on his coat and rushes out without ever having looked at her. She shouts after him.*) I look at you and I see the final triumph of stupidity in the world!

[*The door slams and she returns to just sitting again.* RUTH *comes quickly out of* MAMA's *room.*]

Ruth. Who was that?
Beneatha. Your husband.
Ruth. Where did he go?
Beneatha. Who knows—maybe he has an appointment at U.S. Steel.
Ruth (*anxiously, with frightened eyes*). You didn't say nothing bad to him, did you?

Beneatha. Bad? Say anything bad to him? No—I told him he was a sweet boy and full of dreams and everything is strictly peachy keen, as the ofay kids say!

[MAMA *enters from her bedroom. She is lost, vague, trying to catch hold, to make some sense of her former command of the world, but it still eludes her. A sense of waste overwhelms her gait; a measure of apology rides on her shoulders. She goes to her plant, which has remained on the table, looks at it, picks it up, and takes it to the windowsill and sits it outside, and she stands and looks at it a long moment. Then she closes the window, straightens her body with effort, and turns around to her children.*]

Mama. Well—ain't it a mess in here, though? (*A false cheerfulness, a beginning of something*) I guess we all better stop moping around and get some work done. All this unpacking and everything we got to do. (RUTH *raises her head slowly in response to the sense of the line; and* BENEATHA *in similar manner turns very slowly to look at her mother.*) One of you all better call the moving people and tell 'em not to come.

Ruth. Tell 'em not to come?

Mama. Of course, baby. Ain't no need in 'em coming all the way here and having to go back. They charges for that too. (*She sits down, fingers to her brow, thinking.*) Lord, ever since I was a little girl, I always remembers people saying, "Lena—Lena Eggleston, you aims too high all the time. You needs to slow down and see life a little more like it is. Just slow down some." That's what they always used to say down home—"Lord, that Lena Eggleston is a high-minded thing. She'll get her due one day!"

Ruth. No, Lena . . .

Mama. Me and Big Walter just didn't never learn right.

Ruth. Lena, no! We gotta go. Bennie—tell her . . . (*She rises and crosses to* BENEATHA *with her arms outstretched.* BENEATHA *doesn't respond.*) Tell her we can still move . . . the notes ain't but a hundred and twenty-five a month. We got four grown people in this house—we can work . . .

Mama (*to herself*). Just aimed too high all the time—

Ruth (*turning and going to* MAMA *fast—the words pouring out with urgency and desperation*). Lena—I'll work . . . I'll work twenty hours a day in all the kitchens in Chicago . . . I'll strap my baby on my back if I have to and scrub all the floors in America and wash all the sheets in America if I have to—but we got to MOVE! We got to get OUT OF HERE!!

[MAMA *reaches out absently and pats* RUTH's *hand.*]

Mama. No—I sees things differently now. Been thinking 'bout some of the things we could do to fix this place up some. I seen a secondhand bureau over on Maxwell Street just the other day that could fit right there. (*She points to where the new furniture might go.* RUTH *wanders away from her.*) Would need some new handles on it and then a little varnish and it look like something brand-new. And—we can put up them new curtains in the kitchen . . . Why this place be looking fine. Cheer us all up so that we forget trouble ever come . . . (*To* RUTH) And you could get some nice screens to put up in your room round the baby's bassinet . . . (*She looks at both of them, pleadingly.*) Sometimes you just got to know when to give up some things . . . and hold on to what you got. . . .

[WALTER *enters from the outside, looking spent and leaning against the door, his coat hanging from him.*]

Mama. Where you been, son?
Walter (*breathing hard*). Made a call.
Mama. To who, son?
Walter. To The Man. (*He heads for his room.*)
Mama. What man, baby?
Walter (*stops in the door*). The Man, Mama. Don't you know who The Man is?
Ruth. Walter Lee?
Walter. *The Man.* Like the guys in the streets say—The Man. Captain Boss—Mistuh Charley . . . Old Cap'n Please Mr. Bossman . . .
Beneatha (*suddenly*). Lindner!
Walter. That's right! That's good. I told him to come right over.

Beneatha (*fiercely, understanding*). For what? What do you want to see him for!

Walter (*looking at his sister*). We going to do business with him.

Mama. What you talking 'bout, son?

Walter. Talking 'bout life, Mama. You all always telling me to see life like it is. Well—I laid in there on my back today . . . and I figured it out. Life just like it is. Who gets and who don't get. (*He sits down with his coat on and laughs.*) Mama, you know it's all divided up. Life is. Sure enough. Between the takers and the "tooken." (*He laughs.*) I've figured it out finally. (*He looks around at them.*) Yeah. Some of us always getting "tooken." (*He laughs.*) People like Willy Harris, they don't never get "tooken." And you know why the rest of us do? 'Cause we all mixed up. Mixed up bad. We get to looking 'round for the right and the wrong; and we worry about it and cry about it and stay up nights trying to figure out 'bout the wrong and the right of things all the time . . . And all the time, man, them takers is out there operating, just taking and taking. Willy Harris? Shoot—Willy Harris don't even count. He don't even count in the big scheme of things. But I'll say one thing for old Willy Harris . . . he's taught me something. He's taught me to keep my eye on what counts in this world. Yeah—(*Shouting out a little*) Thanks, Willy!

Ruth. What did you call that man for, Walter Lee?

Walter. Called him to tell him to come on over to the show. Gonna put on a show for the man. Just what he wants to see. You see, Mama, the man came here today and he told us that them people out there where you want us to move—well they so upset they willing to pay us *not* to move! (*He laughs again.*) And—and oh, Mama—you would of been proud of the way me and Ruth and Bennie acted. We told him to get out . . . Lord have mercy! We told the man to get out! Oh, we was some proud folks this afternoon, yeah. (*He lights a cigarette.*) We were still full of that old-time stuff . . .

Ruth (*coming toward him slowly*). You talking 'bout taking them people's money to keep us from moving in that house?

Walter. I ain't just talking 'bout it, baby—I'm telling you that's what's going to happen!

Beneatha. Oh, God! Where is the bottom! Where is the real honest-to-God bottom so he can't go any farther!

Walter. See—that's the old stuff. You and that boy that was here today. You all want everybody to carry a flag and a spear and sing some marching songs, huh? You wanna spend your life looking into things and trying to find the right and the wrong part, huh? Yeah. You know what's going to happen to that boy someday—he'll find himself sitting in a dungeon, locked in forever—and the takers will have the key! Forget it, baby! There ain't no causes—there ain't nothing but taking in this world, and he who takes most is smartest—and it don't make a bit of difference *how*.

Mama. You making something inside me cry, son. Some awful pain inside me.

Walter. Don't cry, Mama. Understand. That white man is going to walk in that door able to write checks for more money than we ever had. It's important to him and I'm going to help him . . . I'm going to put on the show, Mama.

Mama. Son—I come from five generations of people who was slaves and sharecroppers—but ain't nobody in my family never let nobody pay 'em no money that was a way of telling us we wasn't fit to walk the earth. We ain't never been that poor. (*Raising her eyes and looking at him*) We ain't never been that—dead inside.

Beneatha. Well—we are dead now. All the talk about dreams and sunlight that goes on in this house. It's all dead now.

Walter. What's the matter with you all! I didn't make this world! It was give to me this way! Lord, yes, I want me some yachts someday! Yes, I want to hang some real pearls 'round my wife's neck. Ain't she supposed to wear no pearls? Somebody tell me—tell me, who decides which women is suppose to wear pearls in this world. I tell you I am a *man*—and I think my wife should wear some pearls in this world!

[*This last line hangs a good while and* WALTER *begins to move about the room. The word "Man" has penetrated his consciousness; he mumbles it to himself repeatedly between strange agitated pauses as he moves about.*]

Mama. Baby, how you going to feel on the inside?

Walter. Fine! . . . Going to feel fine . . . a man . . .

Mama. You won't have nothing left then, Walter Lee.

Walter (*coming to her*). I'm going to feel fine, Mama. I'm going to look that man in the eyes and say—(*He falters.*)—and say, "All right, Mr. Lindner—(*He falters even more.*)—that's *your* neighborhood out there! You got the right to keep it like you want! You got the right to have it like you want! Just write the check and—the house is yours." And—and I am going to say—(*His voice almost breaks.*) "And you—you people just put the money in my hand and you won't have to live next to this bunch of stinking . . ." (*He straightens up and moves away from his mother, walking around the room.*) And maybe—maybe I'll just get down on my black knees . . . (*He does so;* RUTH *and* BENNIE *and* MAMA *watch him in frozen horror.*) "Captain, Mistuh, Bossman—(*Groveling and grinning and wringing his hands in profoundly anguished imitation of the slow-witted movie stereotype*) A-hee-hee-hee! Oh, yassuh boss! Yassssssuh! Great white—(*Voice breaking, he forces himself to go on.*)—Father, just gi' ussen de money, fo' God's sake, and we's—we's ain't gwine come out deh and dirty up yo' white folks neighborhood . . ." (*He breaks down completely.*) And I'll feel fine! Fine! FINE! (*He gets up and goes into the bedroom.*)

Beneatha. That is not a man. That is nothing but a toothless rat.

Mama. Yes—death done come in this here house. (*She is nodding, slowly, reflectively.*) Done come walking in my house on the lips of my children. You what supposed to be my beginning again. You—what supposed to be my harvest. (*To* BENEATHA) You—you mourning your brother?

Beneatha. He's no brother of mine.

Mama. What you say?

Beneatha. I said that that individual in that room is no brother of mine.

Mama. That's what I thought you said. You feeling like you better than he is today? (BENEATHA *does not answer.*) Yes? What you tell him a minute ago? That he wasn't a man. Yes? You give him up for me? You done wrote his epitaph too—like the rest of the world? Well, who give you the privilege?

Beneatha. Be on my side for once! You saw what he just did, Mama! You saw him—down on his knees. Wasn't it you who taught me to despise any man who would do that? Do what he's going to do?

Mama. Yes—I taught you that. Me and your daddy. But I thought I taught you something else too . . . I thought I taught you to love him.

Beneatha. Love him? There is nothing left to love.

Mama. There is *always* something left to love. And if you ain't learned that, you ain't learned nothing. (*Looking at her*) Have you cried for that boy today? I don't mean for yourself and for the family 'cause we lost the money. I mean for him: what he been through and what it done to him. Child, when do you think is the time to love somebody the most? When they done good and made things easy for everybody? Well then, you ain't through learning—because that ain't the time at all. It's when he's at his lowest and can't believe in hisself 'cause the world done whipped him so! When you starts measuring somebody, measure him right, child, measure him right. Make sure you done taken into account what hills and valleys he come through before he got to wherever he is.

[TRAVIS *bursts into the room at the end of the speech, leaving the door open.*]

Travis. Grandmama—the moving men are downstairs! The truck just pulled up.

Mama (*turning and looking at him*). Are they, baby? They downstairs?

[*She sighs and sits.* LINDNER *appears in the doorway. He peers in and knocks lightly, to gain attention, and comes in. All turn to look at him.*]

Lindner (*hat and briefcase in hand*). Uh—hello . . .

[RUTH *crosses mechanically to the bedroom door and opens it and lets it swing open freely and slowly as the lights come up on* WALTER *within, still in his coat, sitting at the far corner of the room. He looks up and out through the room to* LINDNER.]

Ruth. He's here.

[*A long minute passes and* WALTER *slowly gets up.*]

Lindner (*coming to the table with efficiency, putting his briefcase on the table and starting to unfold papers and unscrew fountain pens*). Well, I certainly was glad to hear from you people. (WALTER *has begun the trek out of the room, slowly and awkwardly, rather like a small boy, passing the back of his sleeve across his mouth from time to time.*) Life can really be so much simpler than people let it be most of the time. Well—with whom do I negotiate? You, Mrs. Younger, or your son here? (MAMA *sits with her hands folded on her lap and her eyes closed as* WALTER *advances.* TRAVIS *goes closer to* LINDNER *and looks at the papers curiously.*) Just some official papers, sonny.

Ruth. Travis, you go downstairs—

Mama (*opening her eyes and looking into* WALTER's). No. Travis, you stay right here. And you make him understand what you doing, Walter Lee. You teach him good. Like Willy Harris taught you. You show where our five generations done come to. (WALTER *looks from her to the boy, who grins at him innocently.*) Go ahead, son—(*She folds her hands and closes her eyes.*) Go ahead.

Walter (*at last crosses to* LINDNER, *who is reviewing the contract*). Well, Mr. Lindner. (BENEATHA *turns away.*) We called you—(*There is a profound, simple groping quality in his speech.*)—because, well, me and my family (*He looks around and shifts from one foot to the other.*) Well—we are very plain people . . .

Lindner. Yes—

Walter. I mean—I have worked as a chauffeur most of my life—and my wife here, she does domestic work in people's kitchens. So does my mother. I mean—we are plain people . . .

Lindner. Yes, Mr. Younger—

Walter (*really like a small boy, looking down at his shoes and then up at the man*). And—uh—well, my father, well, he was a laborer most of his life. . . .

Lindner (*absolutely confused*). Uh, yes—yes, I understand. (*He turns back to the contract.*)

Walter (*a beat; staring at him*). And my father—(*With sudden intensity*) My father almost *beat a man to death* once because this man called him a bad name or something, you know what I mean?

Lindner (*looking up, frozen*). No, no, I'm afraid I don't—

Walter (*a beat. The tension hangs; then* WALTER *steps back from it.*). Yeah. Well—what I mean is that we come from people who had a lot of *pride*. I mean—we are very proud people. And that's my sister over there and she's going to be a doctor—and we are very proud—

Lindner. Well—I am sure that is very nice, but—

Walter. What I am telling you is that we called you over here to tell you that we are very proud and that this—(*Signaling to* TRAVIS) Travis, come here. (TRAVIS *crosses and* WALTER *draws him before him facing the man.*) This is my son, and he makes the sixth generation our family in this country. And we have all thought about your offer—

Lindner. Well, good . . . good—

Walter. And we have decided to move into our house because my father—my father—he earned it for us brick by brick. (MAMA *has her eyes closed and is rocking back and forth as though she were in church, with her head nodding the Amen yes.*) We don't want to make no trouble for nobody or fight no causes, and we will try to be good neighbors. And that's *all* we got to say about that. (*He looks the man absolutely in the eyes.*) We don't want your money. (*He turns and walks away.*)

Lindner (*looking around at all of them*). I take it then—that you have decided to occupy . . .

Beneatha. That's what the man said.

Lindner (*to* MAMA *in her reverie*). Then I would like to appeal to you, Mrs. Younger. You are older and wiser and understand things better I am sure . . .

Mama. I am afraid you don't understand. My son said we was going to move and there ain't nothing left for me to say. (*Briskly*) You know how these young folks is nowadays, mister. Can't do a thing with 'em. (*As he opens his mouth, she rises.*) Goodbye.

Lindner (*folding up his materials*). Well—if you are that final about it . . . there is nothing left for me to say. (*He finishes, almost ignored by the family, who are concentrating on* WALTER LEE. *At the door* LINDNER *halts and looks around.*) I sure hope you people know what you're getting into.

[*He shakes his head and exits.*]

Ruth (*looking around and coming to life*). Well, for God's sake—if the moving men are here—LET'S GET THIS BLESSED FAMILY OUT OF HERE!

Mama (*into action*). Ain't it the truth! Look at all this here mess. Ruth, put Travis' good jacket on him . . . Walter Lee, fix your tie and tuck your shirt in, you look like somebody's hoodlum! Lord have mercy, where is my plant? (*She flies to get it amid the general bustling of the family, who are deliberately trying to ignore the nobility of the past moment.*) You all start on down . . . Travis child, don't go empty-handed . . . Ruth, where did I put that box with my skillets in it? I want to be in charge of it myself . . . I'm going to make us the biggest dinner we ever ate tonight . . . Beneatha, what's the matter with them stockings? Pull them things up, girl . . .

[*The family starts to file out as two moving men appear and begin to carry out the heavier pieces of furniture, bumping into the family as they move about.*]

Beneatha. Mama, Asagai asked me to marry him today and go to Africa—

Mama (*in the middle of her getting-ready activity*). He did? You ain't old enough to marry nobody—(*Seeing the moving men lifting one of her chairs precariously*) Darling, that ain't no bale of cotton, please handle it so we can sit in it again! I had that chair twenty-five years . . .

[*The movers sigh with exasperation and go on with their work.*]

Beneatha (*girlishly and unreasonably trying to pursue the conversation*). To go to Africa, Mama—be a doctor in Africa . . .
Mama (*distracted*). Yes, baby—
Walter. *Africa!* What he want you to go to Africa for?

Beneatha. To practice there . . .

Walter. Girl, if you don't get all them silly ideas out your head! You better marry yourself a man with some loot . . .

Beneatha (*angrily, precisely as in the first scene of the play*). What have you got to do with who I marry!

Walter. Plenty. Now I think George Murchison—

Beneatha. *George Murchison!* I wouldn't marry him if he was Adam and I was Eve!

[WALTER *and* BENEATHA *go out yelling at each other vigorously and the anger is loud and real till their voices diminish.* RUTH *stands at the door and turns to* MAMA *and smiles knowingly.*]

Mama (*fixing her hat at last*). Yeah—they something all right, my children . . .

Ruth. Yeah—they're something. Let's go, Lena.

Mama (*stalling, starting to look around at the house*). Yes—I'm coming. Ruth—

Ruth. Yes?

Mama (*quietly, woman to woman*). He finally come into his manhood today, didn't he? Kind of like a rainbow after the rain . . .

Ruth (*biting her lip lest her own pride explode in front of* MAMA). Yes, Lena.

[WALTER's *voice calls for them raucously.*]

Walter (*offstage*). Y'all come on! These people charges by the hour, you know!

Mama (*waving* RUTH *out vaguely*). All right, honey—go on down. I be down directly.

[RUTH *hesitates, then exits.* MAMA *stands, at last alone in the living room, her plant on the table before her as the lights start to come down. She looks around at all the walls and ceilings and suddenly, despite herself, while the children call below, a great heaving thing rises in her and she puts her fist to her mouth to stifle it, takes a final desperate look, pulls her coat about her, pats her hat, and goes out. The lights dim down. The door opens and she comes back in, grabs her plant, and goes out for the last time.*]

Curtain

CONNECTIONS

A Letter from the Playwright
Lorraine Hansberry

Lorraine Hansberry wrote the following letter to her mother on January 19, 1959, just before A Raisin in the Sun *opened in New Haven, Connecticut.*

Dear Mother,

Well—here we are. I am sitting alone in a nice hotel room in New Haven, Conn. Downstairs, next door in the Shubert Theatre, technicians are putting the finishing touches on a living room that is supposed to be a Chicago living room. Wednesday the curtain goes up at 8 P.M. The next day the New Haven papers will say what they think about our efforts. A great deal of money has been spent and a lot of people have done some hard, hard work, and it may be the beginning of many different careers.

The actors are very good and the director is a very talented man—so if it is a poor show I won't be able to blame a soul but your youngest daughter.

Mama, it is a play that tells the truth about people, Negroes, and life and I think it will help a lot of people to understand how we are just as complicated as they are—and just as mixed up—but above all, that we have among our miserable and downtrodden ranks—people who are the very essence of human dignity. That is what, after all the laughter and tears, the play is supposed to say. I hope it will make you very proud. See you soon. Love to all.

■ ■ ■

Chicago: Southside Summers
from To Be Young, Gifted and Black
Lorraine Hansberry

To Be Young, Gifted and Black, *a collection of Lorraine Hansberry's letters, journals, speeches, and play fragments, was published in 1969, four years after her death. Written at different stages of her development as a writer, they serve as an informal autobiography and leave readers saddened at the loss of so promising a writer. In his introduction to the book, Hansberry's friend James Baldwin wrote, "When so bright a light goes out so early, when so gifted an artist goes so soon, we are left with a sorrow and wonder which speculation cannot assuage." In this excerpt, "Chicago: Southside Summers," Hansberry remembers the city of her birth and childhood.*

1.

For some time now—I think since I was a child—I have been possessed of the desire to put down the stuff of my life. That is a commonplace impulse, apparently, among persons of massive self-interest; sooner or later we all do it. And, I am quite certain, there is only one internal quarrel: how much of the truth to tell? How much, how much, how much! It *is* brutal, in sober uncompromising moments, to reflect on the comedy of concern we all enact when it comes to our precious images!

Even so, when such vanity as propels the writing of such memoirs is examined, certainly one would wish at least to have some boast of social serviceability on one's side. I shall set down in these pages what shall seem to me to be the truth of my life and essences . . . which are to be found, first of all, on the Southside of Chicago, where I was born. . . .

2.

All travelers to my city should ride the elevated trains that race along the back ways of Chicago. The lives you can look into!

I think you could find the tempo of my people on their back porches. The honesty of their living is there in the shabbiness. Scrubbed porches that sag and look their danger. Dirty gray wood steps. And always a line of white and pink clothes scrubbed so well, waving in the dirty wind of the city.

My people are poor. And they are tired. And they are determined to live.

Our Southside is a place apart: each piece of our living is a protest.

3.

STATE OF ILLINOIS
Department of Public Health—Division of Vital Statistics

CERTIFICATE OF BIRTH

PLACE OF BIRTH   Registered No. 21383

County of _____Cook_____   Date of Birth ___May 19, 1930___
_____Chicago_____

Full name of child _____Loraine Hansberry_____

Sex of Child __Female_____   Legitimate ___Yes_____

FATHER   MOTHER

Full Name _Carl A. Hansberry____   Full Name _Nannie Perry_____

Residence _5330 Calumet Ave.__   Residence _5330 Calumet Ave.__

Color _____Negro_ Black_____   Color _____Negro_ Black_____

Age _35____ Years   Age _32____ Years

Birthplace _Glaston, Miss._____   Birthplace _Columbia, Tenn.____

Occupation _U.S. Deputy Marshall_   Occupation _Ward Committeeman

Number of Children of this Mother
(a) Born alive and now living ___4___
(b) Born alive and now dead __0___
(c) Stillborn __0____

4.

I was born May 19, 1930, the last of four children.

Of love and my parents there is little to be written: their relationship to their children was utilitarian. We were fed and housed and dressed and outfitted with more cash than our associates and that was all. We were also vaguely taught certain vague absolutes: that we were better than no one but infinitely superior to everyone; that we were the products of the proudest and most mistreated of the races of man; that there was nothing enormously difficult about life; that one *succeeded* as a matter of course.

Life was not a struggle—it was something that one *did.* One won an argument because, if facts gave out, one invented them—with color! The only sinful people in the world were dull people. And, above all, there were two things which were never to be betrayed: the family and the race. But of love, there was nothing ever said.

If we were sick, we were sternly, impersonally, and carefully nursed and doctored back to health. Fevers, toothaches were attended to with urgency and importance; one always felt *important* in my family. Mother came with a tray to your room with the soup and Vick's salve or gave the enemas in a steaming bathroom. But we were not fondled, any of us— head held to breast, fingers about that head—until we were grown, all of us, and my father died.

At his funeral I at last, in my memory, saw my mother hold her sons that way, and for the first time in her life my sister held me in her arms, I think. We were not a loving people: we were passionate in our hostilities and affinities, but the caress embarrassed us.

We have changed little. . . .

5.

Seven years separated the nearest of my brothers and sisters
and myself; I wear, I am sure, the earmarks of that familial
station to this day. Little has been written or thought, to my
knowledge, about children who occupy that place: the last-
born separated by an uncommon length of time from the
next youngest. I suspect we are probably a race apart.

The last-born is an object toy which comes in years when
brothers and sisters who are seven, ten, twelve years older
are old enough to appreciate it rather than poke out its eyes.
They do not mind diapering you the first two years, but by
the time you are five you are a pest that has to be attended to
in the washroom, taken to the movies, and "sat with" at night.
You are not a person—you are a nuisance who is not particular fun anymore. Consequently, you swiftly learn to play
alone. . . .

6.

My childhood Southside summers were the ordinary city kind,
full of the street games which other rememberers have turned
into fine ballets these days, and rhymes that anticipated what
some people insist on calling modern poetry:

Oh, Mary Mack, Mack, Mack
With the silver buttons, buttons, buttons
All down her back, back, back.
She asked her mother, mother, mother
For fifteen cents, cents, cents
To see the elephant, elephant, elephant
Jump the fence, fence, fence.
Well, he jumped so high, high, high
'Til he touched the sky, sky, sky
And he didn't come back, back, back
'Til the Fourth of Ju—ly, ly, ly!

I remember skinny little Southside bodies by the fives and tens of us panting the delicious hours away:

"May I?"

And the voice of authority: "Yes, you may—you may take one giant step."

One drew in all one's breath and tightened one's fist and pulled the small body against the heavens, stretching, straining all the muscles in the legs to make—one giant step.

It is a long time. One forgets the reason for the game. (For children's games are always explicit in their reasons for being. To play is to win something. Or not to be "it." Or to be high pointer, or outdoer, or, sometimes—just *the winner.* But after a time one forgets.)

Why was it important to take a small step, a teeny step, or the most desired of all—one GIANT step?

A giant step *to where?*

7.

Evenings were spent mainly on the back porches where screen doors slammed in the darkness with those really very special summertime sounds. And, sometimes, when Chicago nights got too steamy, the whole family got into the car and went to the park and slept out in the open on blankets. Those were, of course, the best times of all because the grownups were invariably reminded of having been children in the South and told the best stories then. And it was also cool and sweet to be on the grass and there was usually the scent of freshly cut lemons or melons in the air. Daddy would lie on his back, as fathers must, and explain about how men thought the stars above us came to be and how far away they were.

I never did learn to believe that anything could be as far away as *that.* Especially the stars. . . .

8.

The man that I remember was an educated soul, though I think now, looking back, that it was as much a matter of the physical bearing of my father as his command of information and of thought that left that impression upon me. I know nothing of the "assurance of kings" and will not use that metaphor on account of it. Suffice it to say that my father's enduring image in my mind is that of a man whom kings might have imitated and properly created their own flattering descriptions of. A man who always seemed to be doing something brilliant and/or unusual to such an extent that to be doing something brilliant and/or unusual was the way I assumed fathers behaved.

He digested the laws of the State of Illinois and put them into little booklets. He invented complicated pumps and rail-road devices. He could talk at length on American history and private enterprise (to which he utterly subscribed). And he carried his head in such a way that I was quite certain that there was nothing he was afraid of. Even writing this, how profoundly it shocks my inner senses to realize suddenly that *my father*, like all men, must have known *fear*. . . .

9.

April 23, 1964

To the Editor
The New York Times:

With reference to civil disobedience and the Congress of Racial Equality stall-in:

. . . My father was typical of a generation of Negroes who believed that the "American way" could successfully be made to work to democratize the United States. Thus, twenty-five years ago, he spent a small personal fortune, his considerable talents, and many years of his life fighting, in association with

NAACP attorneys, Chicago's "restrictive covenants" in one of this nation's ugliest ghettos.

That fight also required that our family occupy the disputed property in a hellishly hostile "white neighborhood" in which, literally, howling mobs surrounded our house. One of their missiles almost took the life of the then eight-year-old signer of this letter. My memories of this "correct" way of fighting white supremacy in America include being spat at, cursed, and pummeled in the daily trek to and from school. And I also remember my desperate and courageous mother, patrolling our house all night with a loaded German luger, doggedly guarding her four children, while my father fought the respectable part of the battle in the Washington court.

The fact that my father and the NAACP "won" a Supreme Court decision, in a now famous case which bears his name in the lawbooks, is—ironically—the sort of "progress" our satisfied friends allude to when they presume to deride the more radical means of struggle. The cost, in emotional turmoil, time, and money, which led to my father's early death as a permanently embittered exile in a foreign country when he saw that after such sacrificial efforts the Negroes of Chicago were as ghetto-locked as ever, does not seem to figure in their calculations.

That is the reality that I am faced with when I now read that some Negroes my own age and younger say that we must now lie down in the streets, tie up traffic, do whatever we can—take to the hills with guns if necessary—and fight back. Fatuous people remark these days on our "bitterness." Why, of course we are bitter. The entire situation suggests that the nation be reminded of the too little noted final lines of Langston Hughes' mighty poem:

■■■

What happens to a dream deferred?
    Does it dry up
    Like a raisin in the sun?
    Or fester like a sore—
    And then run?
    Does it stink like rotten meat?
    Or crust and sugar over—
    Like a syrupy sweet?

    Maybe it just sags
    Like a heavy load.

    Or does it explode?
        Sincerely,

    Lorraine Hansberry

■ ■ ■

My Dungeon Shook: Letter to My Nephew on the One Hundredth Anniversary of the Emancipation
from The Fire Next Time
James Baldwin

James Baldwin (1924–1987) was born and raised in New York City's Harlem but spent many years in France. His novels include Go Tell It on the Mountain *(1953) and* Another Country *(1962). Two of Baldwin's plays,* The Amen Corner *(1955) and* Blues for Mister Charlie *(1964), were produced on Broadway. Baldwin is perhaps best known for his collections of autobiographical and critical essays, which include* Notes of a Native Son *(1955),* Nobody Knows My Name: More Notes of a Native Son *(1961), and* The Fire Next Time *(1963).*

The Fire Next Time consists of two parts, "My Dungeon Shook" and "Down at the Cross." In "My Dungeon Shook," written as a letter to his nephew, Baldwin expresses his anger and sorrow at the persistence of racism in the United States and at its destructive impact on both blacks and whites. In "Down at the Cross," which was first published in The New Yorker *in November 1962, Baldwin reflects on religion and race in America.*

Baldwin took the title "My Dungeon Shook" from a traditional spiritual. It alludes to the Biblical story of Paul and Silas (Acts 16), who were imprisoned unjustly and were then freed by an earthquake whose force severed their chains.

Dear James:

I have begun this letter five times and torn it up five times. I keep seeing your face, which is also the face of your father and my brother. Like him, you are tough, dark, vulnerable, moody—with a very definite tendency to sound truculent because you want no one to think you are soft. You may be like your grandfather in this, I don't know, but certainly both

you and your father resemble him very much physically.
Well, he is dead, he never saw you, and he had a terrible life;
he was defeated long before he died because, at the bottom
of his heart, he really believed what white people said about
him. This is one of the reasons that he became so holy. I am
sure that your father has told you something about all that.
Neither you nor your father exhibit any tendency towards
holiness: you really *are* of another era, part of what happened
when the Negro left the land and came into what the late E.
Franklin Frazier called "the cities of destruction." You can
only be destroyed by believing that you really are what the
white world calls a *nigger.* I tell you this because I love you,
and please don't you ever forget it.

I have known both of you all your lives, have carried
your Daddy in my arms and on my shoulders, kissed and
spanked him and watched him learn to walk. I don't know if
you've known anybody from that far back; if you've loved
anybody that long, first as an infant, then as a child, then as a
man, you gain a strange perspective on time and human pain
and effort. Other people cannot see what I see whenever I
look into your father's face, for behind your father's face as it
is today are all those other faces which were his. Let him
laugh and I see a cellar your father does not remember and a
house he does not remember and I hear in his present laughter his laughter as a child. Let him curse and I remember him
falling down the cellar steps, and howling, and I remember,
with pain, his tears, which my hand or your grandmother's so
easily wiped away. But no one's hand can wipe away those
tears he sheds invisibly today, which one hears in his laughter
and in his speech and in his songs. I know what the world
has done to my brother and how narrowly he has survived it.
And I know, which is much worse, and this is the crime of
which I accuse my country and my countrymen, and for
which neither I nor time nor history will ever forgive them,

that they have destroyed and are destroying hundreds of thousands of lives and do not know it and do not want to know it. One can be, indeed one must strive to become, tough and philosophical concerning destruction and death, for this is what most of mankind has been best at, since we have heard of man. (But remember: *most* of mankind is not *all* of mankind.) But it is not permissible that the authors of devastation should also be innocent. It is the innocence which constitutes the crime.

Now, my dear namesake, these innocent and well-meaning people, your countrymen, have caused you to be born under conditions not very far removed from those described for us by Charles Dickens in the London of more than a hundred years ago. (I hear the chorus of the innocents screaming, "No! This is not true! How *bitter* you are!"—but I am writing this letter to *you,* to try to tell you something about how to handle *them,* for most of them do not yet really know that you exist. I *know* the conditions under which you were born, for I was there. Your countrymen were *not* there, and haven't made it yet. Your grandmother was also there, and no one has ever accused her of being bitter. I suggest that the innocents check with her. She isn't hard to find. Your countrymen don't know that *she* exists, either, though she has been working for them all their lives.)

Well, you were born, here you came, something like fourteen years ago; and though your father and mother and grandmother, looking about the streets through which they were carrying you, staring at the walls into which they brought you, had every reason to be heavyhearted, yet they were not. For here you were, Big James, named for me—you were a big baby, I was not—here you were: to be loved. To be loved, baby, hard, at once, and forever, to strengthen you against the loveless world. Remember that: I know how black it looks today, for you. It looked bad that day, too, yes, we were trembling. We have not stopped trembling yet, but if we had not loved each other none of us would have survived. And now you must survive because we love you, and for the sake of your children and your children's children.

This innocent country set you down in a ghetto in which, in fact, it intended that you should perish. Let me spell out precisely what I mean by that, for the heart of the matter is here, and the root of my dispute with my country. You were born where you were born and faced the future that you faced because you were black and *for no other reason.* The limits of your ambition were, thus, expected to be set forever. You were born into a society which spelled out with brutal clarity, and in as many ways as possible, that you were a worthless human being. You were not expected to aspire to excellence: you were expected to make peace with mediocrity. Wherever you have turned, James, in your short time on this earth, you have been told where you could go and what you could do (and *how* you could do it) and where you could live and whom you could marry. I know your countrymen do not agree with me about this, and I hear them saying, "You exaggerate." They do not know Harlem, and I do. So do you. Take no one's word for anything, including mine—but trust your experience. Know whence you came. If you know whence you came, there is really no limit to where you can go. The details and symbols of your life have been deliberately constructed to make you believe what white people say about you. Please try to remember that what they believe, as well as what they do and cause you to endure, does not testify to your inferiority but to their inhumanity and fear. Please try to be clear, dear James, through the storm which rages about your youthful head today, about the reality which lies behind the words *acceptance* and *integration.* There is no reason for you to try to become like white people and there is no basis whatever for their impertinent assumption that *they* must accept *you*. The really terrible thing, old buddy, is that *you* must accept *them*. And I mean that very seriously. You must accept them and accept them with love. For these innocent people have no other hope. They are, in effect, still trapped in a history which they do not understand; and until they understand it, they cannot be released from it. They have had to believe for many years, and for innumerable reasons, that black men are inferior to white men. Many of them, indeed, know better, but, as you will discover, people find it very difficult to act on what they know. To act is to be committed, and to be committed is to be in danger. In this case, the danger, in the minds of most white Americans, is the loss of their identity. Try to imagine how you would feel if you woke up one morning to find the sun shining and all the stars aflame. You would be frightened because it is out of the order of nature. Any upheaval in the universe is terrifying because it so profoundly attacks one's sense of one's own reality. Well, the black man has functioned in the white man's world as a fixed star, as an immovable pillar: and as he moves out of his place, heaven and earth are shaken to their foundations. You, don't be afraid. I said that it was intended that you should perish in the ghetto, perish by never being allowed to go behind the white man's definitions, by never being allowed to spell your proper name. You have, and many of us have, defeated this intention; and, by a terrible law, a terrible paradox, those innocents who believed that your imprisonment made them safe are losing their grasp of reality. But these men are your brothers—your lost, younger brothers. And if the word *integration* means anything, this is what it means: that we, with love, shall force our brothers to see themselves as they are, to cease fleeing from reality and begin to change it. For this is your home, my friend, do not be driven from it; great men have done great things here, and will again, and we can make America what America must become. It will be hard, James, but you come from sturdy, peasant stock, men who picked cotton and dammed rivers and built railroads, and, in the teeth of the most terrifying odds, achieved an unassailable and monumental dignity. You come from a long line of great poets, some of the greatest poets since Homer. One of them said, *The very time I thought I was lost, My dungeon shook and my chains fell off.*

You know, and I know, that the country is celebrating one hundred years of freedom one hundred years too soon. We cannot be free until they are free. God bless you, James, and Godspeed.

Your uncle,
James

■ ■ ■

Home
from Maud Martha
Gwendolyn Brooks

*Gwendolyn Brooks (1917–   ) was born in Kansas but grew up in
Chicago and has been identified with that city for most of her life.
Brooks established her credentials early, with two volumes of poetry,
one of which won a Pulitzer Prize in 1949. In addition to her liter-
ary achievements, Brooks has been honored for her work in behalf
of young black writers.*

"Home" is an excerpt from her novel Maud Martha *(1953), a
series of vignettes about a young woman living in Chicago during
the 1940s and 1950s. Maud Martha is the narrator.*

What had been wanted was this always, this always to last, the
talking softly on this porch, with the snake plant in the jar-
diniere in the southwest corner, and the obstinate slip from
Aunt Eppie's magnificent Michigan fern at the left side of the
friendly door. Mama, Maud Martha, and Helen rocked slowly in
their rocking chairs, and looked at the late afternoon light on
the lawn, and at the emphatic iron of the fence and at the
poplar tree. These things might soon be theirs no longer. Those
shafts and pools of light, the tree, the graceful iron, might soon
be viewed possessively by different eyes.

Papa was to have gone that noon, during his lunch hour, to
the office of the Home Owners' Loan. If he had not succeeded
in getting another extension, they would be leaving this house
in which they had lived for more than fourteen years. There was
little hope. The Home Owners' Loan was hard. They sat, making their plans.

"We'll be moving into a nice flat somewhere," said Mama.
"Somewhere on South Park, or Michigan, or in Washington
Park Court." Those flats, as the girls and Mama knew well, were

burdens on wages twice the size of Papa's. This was not mentioned now.

"They're much prettier than this old house," said Helen. "I have friends I'd just as soon not bring here. And I have other friends that wouldn't come down this far for anything, unless they were in a taxi."

Yesterday, Maud Martha would have attacked her. Tomorrow she might. Today she said nothing. She merely gazed at a little hopping robin in the tree, her tree, and tried to keep the fronts of her eyes dry.

"Well, I do know," said Mama, turning her hands over and over, "that I've been getting tireder and tireder of doing that firing. From October to April, there's firing to be done."

"But lately we've been helping, Harry and I," said Maud Martha. "And sometimes in March and April and in October, and even in November, we could build a little fire in the fireplace. Sometimes the weather was just right for that."

She knew, from the way they looked at her, that this had been a mistake. They did not want to cry.

But she felt that the little line of white, somewhat ridged with smoked purple, and all that cream-shot saffron, would never drift across any western sky except that in back of this house. The rain would drum with as sweet a dullness nowhere but here. The birds on South Park were mechanical birds, no better than the poor caught canaries in those "rich" women's sun parlors.

"It's just going to kill Papa!" burst out Maud Martha. "He loves this house! He *lives* for this house!"

"He lives for us," said Helen. "It's us he loves. He wouldn't want the house, except for us."

"And he'll have us," added Mama, "wherever."

"You know," Helen sighed, "if you want to know the truth, this is a relief. If this hadn't come up, we would have gone on, just dragged on, hanging out here forever."

"It might," allowed Mama, "be an act of God. God may just have reached down, and picked up the reins."

"Yes," Maud Martha cracked in, "that's what you always say—that God knows best."

Her mother looked at her quickly, decided the statement was not suspect, looked away.

Helen saw Papa coming. "There's Papa," said Helen.

They could not tell a thing from the way Papa was walking. It was that same dear little staccato walk, one shoulder down, then the other, then repeat, and repeat. They watched his progress. He passed the Kennedys', he passed the vacant lot, he passed Mrs. Blakemore's. They wanted to hurl themselves over the fence, into the street, and shake the truth out of his collar. He opened his gate—the gate—and still his stride and face told them nothing.

"Hello," he said.

Mama got up and followed him through the front door. The girls knew better than to go in too.

Presently Mama's head emerged. Her eyes were lamps turned on.

"It's all right," she exclaimed. "He got it. It's all over. Everything is all right."

The door slammed shut. Mama's footsteps hurried away.

"I think," said Helen, rocking rapidly, "I think I'll give a party. I haven't given a party since I was eleven. I'd like some of my friends to just casually see that we're homeowners."

2239 North 16th Street

from Sweet Summer:
Growing Up with and Without My Dad
Bebe Moore Campbell

Bebe Moore Campbell (1950–   ) writes for Ebony, Ms., and
The New York Times Book Review. *This piece is an excerpt
from her memoir, set in the Philadelphia of her childhood.
Campbell's story takes place in the late 1950s and early 1960s,
a time of enormous social and political change in America.*

The red bricks of 2239 North 16th Street melded into the
uniformity of look-alike doors, windows, and brownstone-
steps. From the outside our rowhouse looked the same as
any other. When I was a toddler, the similarity was unsettling.
The family story was that my mother and I were out walking
on the street one day when panic rumbled through me.
"Where's our house? Where's our house?" I cried, grabbing
my mother's hand.

My mother walked me to our house, pointed to the
numbers painted next to the door. "Twenty-two thirty-nine,"
she said, slapping the wall. "This is our house."

Much later I learned that the real difference was inside.

In my house there was no morning stubble, no long
johns or Fruit of the Loom on the clothesline, no baritone
hollering for keys that were sitting on the table. There was
no beer in the refrigerator, no ball game on TV, no loud
cussing. After dark the snores that emanated from the bedrooms were subtle, ladylike, little moans really.

Growing up, I could have died from overexposure to
femininity. Women ruled at 2239. A grandmother, a mother,
occasionally an aunt, grown-up girlfriends from at least two
generations, all the time rubbing up against me, fixing my

food, running my bathwater, telling me to sit still and be good in those grown-up, girly-girl voices. Chanel and Prince Matchabelli wafting through the bedrooms. Bubble bath and Jergens came from the bathroom, scents unbroken by after-shave, macho beer breath, a good he-man funk. I remember a house full of 'do rags and rollers, the soft, sweet allure of Dixie peach and bergamot; brown-skinned queens wearing pastel housecoats and worn-out size six-and-a-half flip-flops that slapped softly against the wood as the royal women climbed the stairs at night carrying their paperbacks to bed.

The outside world offered no retreat. School was taught by stern, old-maid white women with age spots and merciless gray eyes; ballet lessons, piano lessons, Sunday school, and choir were all led by colored sisters with hands-on-their-hips attitude who cajoled and screeched in distaff tongues.

And what did they want from me, these Bosoms? Achievement! This desire had nothing to do with the pittance they collected from the Philadelphia Board of Education or the few dollars my mother paid them. Pushing little colored girls forward was in their blood. They made it clear: a life of white picket fences and teas was for other girls to aspire to. I was to *do* something. And if I didn't climb willingly up their ladder, they'd drag me to the top. Rap my knuckles hard for not practicing. Make me lift my leg until I wanted to die. Stay after school and write "I will listen to the teacher" five hun-dred times. They were not playing. "Obey them," my mother commanded.

When I entered 2B—the Philadelphia school system divided grades into A and B—in September 1957, I sensed immediately that Miss Bradley was not a woman to be chal-lenged. She looked like one of those evil old spinsters Shirley Temple was always getting shipped off to live with; she was kind of hefty, but so tightly corseted that if she happened to grab you or if you fell against her during recess, it felt as if you were bouncing into a steel wall. In reality she was a

sweet lady who was probably a good five years past her
retirement age when I wound up in her class. Miss Bradley
remained at Logan for one reason and one reason only: she
was dedicated. She wanted her students to learn! learn! learn!
Miss Bradley was halfway sick, hacking and coughing her
lungs out through every lesson, spitting the phlegm into fluffy
white tissues from the box on her desk, but she was *never*
absent. Each day at three o'clock she kissed each one of her
"little pupils" on the cheek, sending a faint scent of Emeraude
home with us. Her rules for teaching children seemed to be:
Love them; discipline them; reward them; and make sure they
are clean.

Every morning she ran a hygiene check on the entire
class. She marched down the aisle like a stormtrooper, rummaging through the ears of hapless students, checking for
embedded wax. She looked under our fingernails for dirt. Too
bad on you if she found any. Once she made David, a
stringy-haired white boy who thought Elvis Presley was a living deity and who was the most notorious booger-eater in the
entire school, go to the nurse's office to have the dirt cleaned
from under his fingernails. Everybody knew that what was
under David's fingernails was most likely dried-up boogies
and not dirt, but nobody said anything.

If she was death on dirt and earwax, Miss Bradley's spe-
cialty was head-lice patrol. Down the aisles she stomped in
her black Enna Jettick shoes, stopping at each student to part
strands of blond, brown, or dark hair, looking for cooties.
Miss Bradley would flip through plaits, curls, kinks—the
woman was relentless. I always passed inspection. Nana put
enough Nu Nile in my hair to suffocate any living creature
that had the nerve to come tipping up on my scalp. Nu Nile
was the official cootie killer. I was clean, wax-free, bug-free,
and smart. The folder inside my desk contained a stack of
spelling and arithmetic papers with A's emblazoned across the
top, gold stars in the corner. Miss Bradley always called on

me. She sent me to run errands for her too. I was her pet.

When Mrs. Clark, my piano teacher and my mother's good friend, told my mother that Logan Elementary School was accepting children who didn't live in the neighborhood, my mother immediately enrolled Michael and later me. "It's not crowded and it's mixed," she told a nodding, smiling Nana. The fact that Logan was integrated was the main reason Michael and I were sent there. Nana and Mommy, like most upwardly mobile colored women, believed that to have the same education as a white child was the first step up the rocky road to success. This viewpoint was buttressed by the fact that George Washington Carver, my neighborhood school, was severely overcrowded. Logan was just barely integrated, with only a handful of black kids thrown in with hordes of square-jawed, pale-eyed second-generation Ukrainians whose immigrant parents and grandparents populated the neighborhood near the school. There were a few dark-haired Jews and aristocratic-looking WASPs too. My first day in kindergarten it was Nana who enthusiastically grabbed Michael's and my hands, pulling us away from North Philly's stacked-up rowhouses, from the hucksters whose wagons bounced down the streets with trucks full of ripe fruits and vegetables, from the street-corner singers and jitterbugs who filled my block with all-day doo-wahs. It was Nana who resolutely walked me past the early-morning hordes of colored kids heading two blocks away to Carver Elementary School, Nana who pulled me by the hand and led me in another direction.

We went underground at the Susquehanna and Dauphin subway station, leaving behind the unremitting asphalt and bricks and the bits of paper strewn in the streets above us. We emerged at Logan station, where sunlight, brilliant red and pink roses and yellow chrysanthemums, and neatly clipped lawns and clean streets startled me. There were robins and blue jays flying overhead. The only birds in my neighborhood were sparrows and pigeons. Delivering me at the schoolyard,

Nana firmly cupped my chin with her hand as she bent down to instruct me. "Your mother's sending you up here to learn, so you do everything your teacher tells you to, okay?" To Michael she turned and said, "You're not up here to be a monkey on a stick." Then to both of us: "Don't talk. Listen. Act like you've got some home training. You've got as much brains as anybody up here. Do you know that? All right now. Make Nana proud of you."

A month after I returned from Pasquotank County, I sat in Miss Bradley's classroom on a rainy Monday watching her write spelling words on the blackboard. The harsh sccurr, sccurr of Miss Bradley's chalk and the tinny sound the rain made against the window took my mind to faraway places. . . .

Two seats ahead of me was Leonard, a lean colored boy from West Philly who always wore suits and ties to school, waving his hand like a crazy man. A showoff if ever there was one.

I was bored that day. I looked around at the walls. Miss Bradley had decorated the room with pictures of the ABCs in cursive. Portraits of the presidents were hanging in a row on one wall above the blackboard. On the bulletin board there was a display of the Russian satellite, *Sputnik I,* and the American satellite, *Explorer I.* Miss Bradley was satellite-crazy. She thought it was just wonderful that America was in the "space race" and she constantly filled our heads with space fantasies. "Boys and girls," she told us, "one day man will walk on the moon." In the far corner on another bulletin board there was a Thanksgiving scene of turkeys and pilgrims. And stuck in the corner was a picture of Sacajawea. Sacajawea, Indian Woman Guide. I preferred looking at Sacajawea over satellites any day.

Thinking about the bubble gum that lay in my pocket, I decided to sneak a piece, even though gum chewing was strictly forbidden. I rarely broke the rules. Could anyone hear the loud drumming of my heart, I wondered, as I slid my hand into my skirt pocket and felt for the Double Bubble? I peeked cautiously to either side of me. Then I managed to unwrap it without even rustling the paper; I drew my hand to my lips, coughed and popped the gum in my mouth. Ahhh! Miss Bradley's back was to the class. I chomped down hard on the Double Bubble. Miss Bradley turned around. I quickly packed the gum under my tongue. My hands were folded on top of my desk. "Who can give me a sentence for 'birthday'?" Leonard just about went nuts. Miss Bradley ignored him, which she did a lot. "Sandra," Miss Bradley called.

A petite white girl rose obediently. I liked Sandra. She had shared her crayons with me once when I left mine at home. I remember her drawing: a white house with smoke coming out of the chimney, a little girl with yellow hair like hers, a mommy, a daddy, a little boy, and a dog standing in front of the house in a yard full of flowers. Her voice was crystal clear when she spoke. There were smiles in that voice. She said, "My father made me a beautiful dollhouse for my birthday."

The lump under my tongue was suddenly a stone and when I swallowed, the taste was bitter. I coughed into a piece of tablet paper, spit out the bubble gum, and crumpled up the wad and pushed it inside my desk. The center of my chest was burning. I breathed deeply and slowly. Sandra sat down as demurely as a princess. She crossed her ankles. Her words came back to me in a rush. "Muuuy fatha made me a bee-yoo-tee-ful dollhouse." Miss Bradley said, "Very good," and moved on to the next word. Around me hands were waving, waving. Pick me! Pick me! Behind me I could hear David softly crooning, "You ain't nothin' but a hound dog, cryin' all the time." Sometimes he would stick his head inside his desk, sing Elvis songs, and pick his boogies at the same time. Somebody was jabbing pins in my chest. Ping! Ping! Ping! I wanted to holler, "Yowee! Stop!" as loud as I could, but I pressed my lips together hard.

"Now who can give me a sentence?" Miss Bradley asked. I put my head down on my desk and when Miss Bradley asked me what was wrong I told her that I didn't feel well and that I didn't want to be chosen. When Leonard collected the homework, I shoved mine at him so hard all the papers he was carrying fell on the floor.

Bile was still clogging my throat when Miss Bradley sent me into the cloakroom to get my lunchbox. The rule was, only one student in the cloakroom at a time. When the second one came in, the first one had to leave. I was still rummaging around in my bookbag when I saw Sandra.

"Miss Bradley said for you to come out," she said. She was smiling. That dollhouse girl was always smiling. I glared at her.

"Leave when I get ready to," I said, my words full of venom.

Sandra's eyes darted around in confusion. "Miss Bradley said . . ." she began again, still trying to smile as if she expected somebody to crown her Miss America or something and come take her picture any minute.

In my head a dam broke. Terrible waters rushed out. "I don't care about any Miss Bradley. If she messes with me I'll, I'll . . . I'll take my butcher knife and stab her until she bleeds." What I lacked in props I made up for in drama. My balled-up hand swung menacingly in the air. I aimed the invisible dagger toward Sandra. Her Miss America smile faded instantly. Her eyes grew round and frightened as she blinked rapidly. "Think I won't, huh? Huh?" I whispered, enjoying my meanness, liking the scared look on Sandra's face. Scaredy cat! Muuuy fatha made me a bee-yoo-tee-ful dollhouse. "What do you think about that?" I added viciously, looking into her eyes to see the total effect of my daring words.

But Sandra wasn't looking at me. Upon closer inspection, I realized that she was looking *over* me with sudden relief in her face. I turned to see what was so interesting, and my chin

jammed smack into the Emeraude-scented iron bosom of
Miss Bradley. Even as my mind scrambled for an excuse,
I knew I was lost.

Miss Bradley had a look of horror on her face. For a
minute she didn't say anything, just stood there looking as
though someone had slapped her across the face. Sandra
didn't say anything. I didn't move. Finally, "Would you mind
repeating what you just said, Bebe."

"I didn't say anything, Miss Bradley." I could feel my
dress sticking to my body.

"Sandra, what did Bebe say?"

Sandra was crying softly, little delicate tears streaming
down her face. For just a second she paused, giving a tiny
shudder. I rubbed my ear vigorously, thinking, "Oh, please . . ."

"She said, she said, if you bothered with her she would
cut you with her knife."

"Unh unh, Miss Bradley, I didn't say that. I didn't. I didn't
say anything like that."

Miss Bradley's gray eyes penetrated mine. She locked me
into her gaze until I looked down at the floor. Then she
looked at Sandra.

"Bebe, you and I had better go see the principal."

The floor blurred. The principal!! Jennie G., the students
called her with awe and fear. As Miss Bradley wrapped her
thick knuckles around my forearm and dutifully steered me
from the cloakroom and out the classroom door, I completely
lost what little cool I had left. I began to cry, a jerky, hic-
cuping, snot-filled cry for mercy. "I didn't say it. I didn't say
it," I moaned.

Miss Bradley was nonplussed. Dedication and duty over-
ruled compassion. Always. "Too late for that now," she said
grimly.

Jennie G.'s office was small, neat, and dim. The principal
was dwarfed by the large brown desk she sat behind, and
when she stood up she wasn't much bigger than I. But she

was big enough to make me tremble as I stood in front of her, listening to Miss Bradley recount the sordid details of my downfall. Jennie G. was one of those pale, pale vein-showing white women. She had a vocabulary of about six horrible phrases, designed to send chills of despair down the spine of any young transgressor. Phrases like "We'll just see about that" or "Come with me, young lady," spoken ominously. Her face was impassive as she listened to Miss Bradley. I'd been told that she had a six-foot paddle in her office used solely to beat young transgressors. Suppose she tried to beat me? My heart gave a lurch. I tugged rapidly at my ears. I longed to suck my thumb.

"Well, Bebe, I think we'll have to call your mother."

My mother! I wanted the floor to swallow me up and take me whole. My mother! As Jennie G. dialed the number, I envisioned my mother's face, clouded with disappointment and shame. I started crying again as I listened to the principal telling my mother what had happened. They talked for a pretty long time. When she hung up, ole Jennie G. flipped through some papers on her desk before looking at me sternly.

"You go back to class and watch your mouth, young lady."

As I was closing the door to her office I heard her say to Miss Bradley, "What can you expect?"

■ ■ ■

Everything That Rises Must Converge
Flannery O'Connor

*Flannery O'Connor (1925–1964), who was born in the South
and spent most of her life there, was famous for her sardonic wit.
Her stories blend the comic and the tragic and are at once humor-
ous and disconcerting. In this story, written in 1959, O'Connor
takes an ironic look at the difficult transition from segregation to
desegregation.*

Her doctor had told Julian's mother that she must lose twenty
pounds on account of her blood pressure, so on Wednesday
nights Julian had to take her downtown on the bus for a
reducing class at the Y. The reducing class was designed for
working girls over fifty, who weighed from 165 to 200
pounds. His mother was one of the slimmer ones, but she
said ladies did not tell their age or weight. She would not ride
the buses by herself at night since they had been integrated,
and because the reducing class was one of her few pleasures,
necessary for her health, and *free,* she said Julian could at
least put himself out to take her, considering all she did for
him. Julian did not like to consider all she did for him, but
every Wednesday night he braced himself and took her.

She was almost ready to go, standing before the hall mirror, putting on her hat, while he, his hands behind him,
appeared pinned to the door frame, waiting like Saint
Sebastian for the arrows to begin piercing him. The hat was
new and had cost her seven dollars and a half. She kept saying, "Maybe I shouldn't have paid that for it. No, I shouldn't
have. I'll take it off and return it tomorrow. I shouldn't have
bought it."

Julian raised his eyes to heaven. "Yes, you should have
bought it," he said. "Put it on and let's go." It was a hideous
hat. A purple velvet flap came down on one side of it and

stood up on the other; the rest of it was green and looked like a cushion with the stuffing out. He decided it was less comical than jaunty and pathetic. Everything that gave her pleasure was small and depressed him.

She lifted the hat one more time and set it down slowly on top of her head. Two wings of gray hair protruded on either side of her florid face, but her eyes, sky-blue, were as innocent and untouched by experience as they must have been when she was ten. Were it not that she was a widow who had struggled fiercely to feed and clothe and put him through school and who was supporting him still, "until he got on his feet," she might have been a little girl that he had to take to town.

"It's all right, it's all right," he said. "Let's go." He opened the door himself and started down the walk to get her going. The sky was a dying violet and the houses stood out darkly against it, bulbous liver-colored monstrosities of a uniform ugliness though no two were alike. Since this had been a fashionable neighborhood forty years ago, his mother persisted in thinking they did well to have an apartment in it. Each house had a narrow collar of dirt around it in which sat, usually, a grubby child. Julian walked with his hands in his pockets, his head down and thrust forward and his eyes glazed with the determination to make himself completely numb during the time he would be sacrificed to her pleasure.

The door closed and he turned to find the dumpy figure, surmounted by the atrocious hat, coming toward him. "Well," she said, "you only live once and paying a little more for it, I at least won't meet myself coming and going."

"Someday I'll start making money," Julian said gloomily —he knew he never would—"and you can have one of those jokes whenever you take the fit." But first they would move. He visualized a place where the nearest neighbors would be three miles away on either side.

"I think you're doing fine," she said, drawing on her gloves. "You've only been out of school a year. Rome wasn't built in a day."

She was one of the few members of the Y reducing class who arrived in hat and gloves and who had a son who had been to college. "It takes time," she said, "and the world is in such a mess. This hat looked better on me than any of the others, though when she brought it out I said, 'Take that thing back. I wouldn't have it on my head,' and she said, 'Now wait till you see it on,' and when she put it on me, I said, 'We-ull,' and she said, 'If you ask me, that hat does something for you and you do something for the hat, and besides,' she said, 'with that hat, you won't meet yourself coming and going.'"

Julian thought he could have stood his lot better if she had been selfish, if she had been an old hag who drank and screamed at him. He walked along, saturated in depression, as if in the midst of his martyrdom he had lost his faith. Catching sight of his long, hopeless, irritated face, she stopped suddenly with a grief-stricken look, and pulled back on his arm. "Wait on me," she said. "I'm going back to the house and take this thing off and tomorrow I'm going to return it. I was out of my head. I can pay the gas bill with that seven-fifty."

He caught her arm in a vicious grip. "You are not going to take it back," he said. "I like it."

"Well," she said, "I don't think I ought . . ."

"Shut up and enjoy it," he muttered, more depressed than ever.

"With the world in the mess it's in," she said, "it's a wonder we can enjoy anything. I tell you, the bottom rail is on the top."

Julian sighed.

"Of course," she said, "if you know who you are, you

▪▪▪

can go anywhere." She said this every time he took her to the reducing class. "Most of them in it are not our kind of people," she said, "but I can be gracious to anybody. I know who I am."

"They don't give a damn for your graciousness," Julian said savagely. "Knowing who you are is good for one generation only. You haven't the foggiest idea where you stand now or who you are."

She stopped and allowed her eyes to flash at him. "I most certainly do know who I am," she said, "and if you don't know who you are, I'm ashamed of you."

"Oh hell," Julian said.

"Your great-grandfather was a former governor of this state," she said. "Your grandfather was a prosperous landowner. Your grandmother was a Godhigh."

"Will you look around you," he said tensely, "and see where you are now?" and he swept his arm jerkily out to indicate the neighborhood, which the growing darkness at least made less dingy.

"You remain what you are," she said. "Your great-grandfather had a plantation and two hundred slaves."

"There are no more slaves," he said irritably.

"They were better off when they were," she said. He groaned to see that she was off on that topic. She rolled onto it every few days like a train on an open track. He knew every stop, every junction, every swamp along the way, and knew the exact point at which her conclusion would roll majestically into the station: "It's ridiculous. It's simply not realistic. They should rise, yes, but on their own side of the fence."

"Let's skip it," Julian said.

"The ones I feel sorry for," she said, "are the ones that are half white. They're tragic."

"Will you skip it?"

"Suppose we were half white. We would certainly have mixed feelings."

"I have mixed feelings now," he groaned.

"Well let's talk about something pleasant," she said. "I remember going to Grandpa's when I was a little girl. Then the house had double stairways that went up to what was really the second floor—all the cooking was done on the first. I used to like to stay down in the kitchen on account of the way the walls smelled. I would sit with my nose pressed against the plaster and take deep breaths. Actually the place belonged to the Godhighs but your grandfather Chestny paid the mortgage and saved it for them. They were in reduced circumstances," she said, "but reduced or not, they never forgot who they were."

"Doubtless that decayed mansion reminded them," Julian muttered. He never spoke of it without contempt or thought of it without longing. He had seen it once when he was a child before it had been sold. The double stairways had rotted and been torn down. Negroes were living in it. But it remained in his mind as his mother had known it. It appeared in his dreams regularly. He would stand on the wide porch, listening to the rustle of oak leaves, then wander through the high-ceilinged hall into the parlor that opened onto it and gaze at the worn rugs and faded draperies. It occurred to him that it was he, not she, who could have appreciated it. He preferred its threadbare elegance to anything he could name and it was because of it that all the neighborhoods they had lived in had been a torment to him—whereas she had hardly known the difference. She called her insensitivity "being adjustable."

"And I remember the old darky who was my nurse, Caroline. There was no better person in the world. I've always had a great respect for my colored friends," she said. "I'd do anything in the world for them and they'd . . ."

"Will you for God's sake get off that subject?" Julian

said. When he got on a bus by himself, he made it a point to sit down beside a Negro, in reparation as it were for his mother's sins.

"You're mighty touchy tonight," she said. "Do you feel all right?"

"Yes I feel all right," he said. "Now lay off."

She pursed her lips. "Well, you certainly are in a vile humor," she observed. "I just won't speak to you at all."

They had reached the bus stop. There was no bus in sight and Julian, his hands still jammed in his pockets and his head thrust forward, scowled down the empty street. The frustration of having to wait on the bus as well as ride on it began to creep up his neck like a hot hand. The presence of his mother was borne in upon him as she gave a pained sigh. He looked at her bleakly. She was holding herself very erect under the preposterous hat, wearing it like a banner of her imaginary dignity. There was in him an evil urge to break her spirit. He suddenly unloosened his tie and pulled it off and put it in his pocket.

She stiffened. "Why must you look like *that* when you take me to town?" she said. "Why must you deliberately embarrass me?"

"If you'll never learn where you are," he said, "you can at least learn where I am."

"You look like a—thug," she said.

"Then I must be one," he murmured.

"I'll just go home," she said. "I will not bother you. If you can't do a little thing like that for me . . ."

Rolling his eyes upward, he put his tie back on. "Restored to my class," he muttered. He thrust his face toward her and hissed, "True culture is in the mind, the *mind,*" he said, and tapped his head, "the mind."

"It's in the heart," she said, "and in how you do things and how you do things is because of who you *are.*"

"Nobody in the damn bus cares who you are."

"I care who I am," she said icily.

The lighted bus appeared on top of the next hill and as it approached, they moved out into the street to meet it. He put his hand under her elbow and hoisted her up on the creaking step. She entered with a little smile, as if she were going into a drawing room where everyone had been waiting for her. While he put in the tokens, she sat down on one of the broad front seats for three which faced the aisle. A thin woman with protruding teeth and long yellow hair was sitting on the end of it. His mother moved up beside her and left room for Julian beside herself. He sat down and looked at the floor across the aisle where a pair of thin feet in red and white canvas sandals were planted.

His mother immediately began a general conversation meant to attract anyone who felt like talking. "Can it get any hotter?" she said and removed from her purse a folding fan, black with a Japanese scene on it, which she began to flutter before her.

"I reckon it might could," the woman with the protruding teeth said, "but I know for a fact my apartment couldn't get no hotter."

"It must get the afternoon sun," his mother said. She sat forward and looked up and down the bus. It was half filled. Everybody was white. "I see we have the bus to ourselves," she said. Julian cringed.

"For a change," said the woman across the aisle, the owner of the red and white canvas sandals. "I come on one the other day and they were thick as fleas—up front and all through."

"The world is in a mess everywhere," his mother said. "I don't know how we've let it get in this fix."

"What gets my goat is all those boys from good families stealing automobile tires," the woman with the protruding teeth said. "I told my boy, I said you may not be rich but you been raised right and if I ever catch you in any such mess, they can send you on to the reformatory. Be exactly where you belong."

"Training tells," his mother said. "Is your boy in high school?"

"Ninth grade," the woman said.

"My son just finished college last year. He wants to write but he's selling typewriters until he gets started," his mother said.

The woman leaned forward and peered at Julian. He threw her such a malevolent look that she subsided against the seat. On the floor across the aisle there was an abandoned newspaper. He got up and got it and opened it out in front of him. His mother discreetly continued the conversation in a lower tone but the woman across the aisle said in a loud voice, "Well that's nice. Selling typewriters is close to writing. He can go right from one to the other."

"I tell him," his mother said, "that Rome wasn't built in a day."

Behind the newspaper Julian was withdrawing into the inner compartment of his mind where he spent most of his time. This was a kind of mental bubble in which he established himself when he could not bear to be a part of what was going on around him. From it he could see out and judge but in it he was safe from any kind of penetration from without. It was the only place where he felt free of the general idiocy of his fellows. His mother had never entered it but from it he could see her with absolute clarity.

The old lady was clever enough and he thought that if she had started from any of the right premises, more might have been expected of her. She lived according to the laws of her own fantasy world, outside of which he had never seen her set foot. The law of it was to sacrifice herself for him after she had first created the necessity to do so by making a mess of things. If he had permitted her sacrifices, it was only because her lack of foresight had made them necessary. All of her life had been a struggle to act like a Chestny without the Chestny goods, and to give him everything she thought a Chestny ought to have; but since, said she, it was fun to struggle, why complain? And when you had won, as she had won, what fun to look back on the hard times! He could not forgive her that she had enjoyed the struggle and that she thought *she* had won.

What she meant when she said she had won was that she had brought him up successfully and had sent him to college and that he had turned out so well—good looking (her teeth had gone unfilled so that his could be straightened), intelligent (he realized he was too intelligent to be a success), and with a future ahead of him (there was of course no future ahead of him). She excused his gloominess on the grounds that he was still growing up and his radical ideas on his lack of practical experience. She said he didn't yet know a thing about "life," that he hadn't even entered the real world— when already he was as disenchanted with it as a man of fifty.

The further irony of all this was that in spite of her, he had turned out so well. In spite of going to only a third-rate college, he had, on his own initiative, come out with a first-rate education; in spite of growing up dominated by a small mind, he had ended up with a large one; in spite of all her foolish views, he was free of prejudice and unafraid to face facts. Most miraculous of all, instead of being blinded by love for her as she was for him, he had cut himself emotionally free of her and could see her with complete objectivity. He was not dominated by his mother.

The bus stopped with a sudden jerk and shook him from his meditation. A woman from the back lurched forward with little steps and barely escaped falling in his newspaper as she righted herself. She got off and a large Negro got on. Julian

kept his paper lowered to watch. It gave him a certain satisfaction to see injustice in daily operation. It confirmed his
view that with a few exceptions there was no one worth
knowing within a radius of three hundred miles. The Negro
was well dressed and carried a briefcase. He looked around
and then sat down on the other end of the seat where the
woman with the red and white canvas sandals was sitting. He
immediately unfolded a newspaper and obscured himself
behind it. Julian's mother's elbow at once prodded insistently
into his ribs. "Now you see why I won't ride on these buses
by myself," she whispered.

The woman with the red and white canvas sandals had
risen at the same time the Negro sat down and had gone further back in the bus and taken the seat of the woman who
had got off. His mother leaned forward and cast her an
approving look.

Julian rose, crossed the aisle, and sat down in the place
of the woman with the canvas sandals. From this position, he
looked serenely across at his mother. Her face had turned an
angry red. He stared at her, making his eyes the eyes of a
stranger. He felt his tension suddenly lift as if he had openly
declared war on her.

He would have liked to get in conversation with the
Negro and to talk with him about art or politics or any subject that would be above the comprehension of those around
them, but the man remained entrenched behind his paper.
He was either ignoring the change of seating or had never
noticed it. There was no way for Julian to convey his sympathy.

His mother kept her eyes fixed reproachfully on his face.
The woman with the protruding teeth was looking at him
avidly as if he were a type of monster new to her.

"Do you have a light?" he asked the Negro.

Without looking away from his paper, the man reached in

his pocket and handed him a packet of matches.

"Thanks," Julian said. For a moment he held the matches foolishly. A NO SMOKING sign looked down upon him from over the door. This alone would not have deterred him; he had no cigarettes. He had quit smoking some months before because he could not afford it. "Sorry," he muttered and handed back the matches. The Negro lowered the paper and gave him an annoyed look. He took the matches and raised the paper again.

His mother continued to gaze at him but she did not take advantage of his momentary discomfort. Her eyes retained their battered look. Her face seemed to be unnaturally red, as if her blood pressure had risen. Julian allowed no glimmer of sympathy to show on his face. Having got the advantage, he wanted desperately to keep it and carry it through. He would have liked to teach her a lesson that would last her a while, but there seemed no way to continue the point. The Negro refused to come out from behind his paper.

Julian folded his arms and looked stolidly before him, facing her but as if he did not see her, as if he had ceased to recognize her existence. He visualized a scene in which, the bus having reached their stop, he would remain in his seat and when she said, "Aren't you going to get off?" he would look at her as at a stranger who had rashly addressed him. The corner they got off on was usually deserted, but it was well lighted and it would not hurt her to walk by herself the four blocks to the Y. He decided to wait until the time came and then decide whether or not he would let her get off by herself. He would have to be at the Y at ten to bring her back, but he could leave her wondering if he was going to show up. There was no reason for her to think she could always depend on him.

He retired again into the high-ceilinged room sparsely settled with large pieces of antique furniture. His soul expanded momentarily but then he became aware of his mother across from him and the vision shriveled. He studied her coldly. Her feet in little pumps dangled like a child's and did not quite reach the floor. She was training on him an exaggerated look of reproach. He felt completely detached from her. At that moment he could with pleasure have slapped her as he would have slapped a particularly obnoxious child in his charge.

He began to imagine various unlikely ways by which he could teach her a lesson. He might make friends with some distinguished Negro professor or lawyer and bring him home to spend the evening. He would be entirely justified but her blood pressure would rise to 300. He could not push her to the extent of making her have a stroke, and moreover, he had never been successful at making any Negro friends. He had tried to strike up an acquaintance on the bus with some of the better types, with ones that looked like professors or ministers or lawyers. One morning he had sat down next to a distinguished-looking dark brown man who had answered his questions with a sonorous solemnity but who had turned out to be an undertaker. Another day he had sat down beside a cigar-smoking Negro with a diamond ring on his finger, but after a few stilted pleasantries, the Negro had rung the buzzer and risen, slipping two lottery tickets into Julian's hand as he climbed over him to leave.

He imagined his mother lying desperately ill and his being able to secure only a Negro doctor for her. He toyed with that idea for a few minutes and then dropped it for a momentary vision of himself participating as a sympathizer in a sit-in demonstration. This was possible but he did not linger with it. Instead, he approached the ultimate horror. He brought home a beautiful suspiciously Negroid woman. Prepare yourself, he said. There is nothing you can do about it. This is the woman I've chosen. She's intelligent, dignified,

even good, and she's suffered and she hasn't thought it *fun*.
Now persecute us, go ahead and persecute us. Drive her out
of here, but remember, you're driving me too. His eyes were
narrowed and through the indignation he had generated, he
saw his mother across the aisle, purple-faced, shrunken to the
dwarflike proportions of her moral nature, sitting like a
mummy beneath the ridiculous banner of her hat.

He was tilted out of his fantasy again as the bus stopped.
The door opened with a sucking hiss and out of the dark a
large, gaily dressed, sullen-looking colored woman got on
with a little boy. The child, who might have been four, had
on a short plaid suit and a Tyrolean hat with a blue feather in
it. Julian hoped that he would sit down beside him and that
the woman would push in beside his mother. He could think
of no better arrangement.

As she waited for her tokens, the woman was surveying
the seating possibilities—he hoped with the idea of sitting
where she was least wanted. There was something familiar-
looking about her but Julian could not place what it was. She
was a giant of a woman. Her face was set not only to meet
opposition but to seek it out. The downward tilt of her large
lower lip was like a warning sign: DON'T TAMPER WITH ME.
Her bulging figure was encased in a green crepe dress and
her feet overflowed in red shoes. She had on a hideous hat. A
purple velvet flap came down on one side of it and stood up
on the other; the rest of it was green and looked like a cushion with the stuffing out. She carried a mammoth red pocketbook that bulged throughout as if it were stuffed with rocks.

To Julian's disappointment, the little boy climbed up on
the empty seat beside his mother. His mother lumped all children, black and white, into the common category, "cute," and
she thought little Negroes were on the whole cuter than little
white children. She smiled at the little boy as he climbed on
the seat.

Meanwhile the woman was bearing down upon the empty seat beside Julian. To his annoyance, she squeezed herself into it. He saw his mother's face change as the woman settled herself next to him and he realized with satisfaction that this was more objectionable to her than it was to him. Her face seemed almost gray and there was a look of dull recognition in her eyes, as if suddenly she had sickened at some awful confrontation. Julian saw that it was because she and the woman had, in a sense, swapped sons. Though his mother would not realize the symbolic significance of this, she would feel it. His amusement showed plainly on his face.

The woman next to him muttered something unintelligible to herself. He was conscious of a kind of bristling next to him, a muted growling like that of an angry cat. He could not see anything but the red pocketbook upright on the bulging green thighs. He visualized the woman as she had stood waiting for her tokens—the ponderous figure, rising from the red shoes upward over the solid hips, the mammoth bosom, the haughty face, to the green and purple hat.

His eyes widened.

The vision of the two hats, identical, broke upon him with the radiance of a brilliant sunrise. His face was suddenly lit with joy. He could not believe that Fate had thrust upon his mother such a lesson. He gave a loud chuckle so that she would look at him and see that he saw. She turned her eyes on him slowly. The blue in them seemed to have turned a bruised purple. For a moment he had an uncomfortable sense of her innocence, but it lasted only a second before principle rescued him. Justice entitled him to laugh. His grin hardened until it said to her as plainly as if he were saying aloud: Your punishment exactly fits your pettiness. This should teach you a permanent lesson.

Her eyes shifted to the woman. She seemed unable to

bear looking at him and to find the woman preferable. He became conscious again of the bristling presence at his side. The woman was rumbling like a volcano about to become active. His mother's mouth began to twitch slightly at one corner. With a sinking heart, he saw incipient signs of recovery on her face and realized that this was going to strike her suddenly as funny and was going to be no lesson at all. She kept her eyes on the woman and an amused smile came over her face as if the woman were a monkey that had stolen her hat. The little Negro was looking up at her with large fascinated eyes. He had been trying to attract her attention for some time.

"Carver!" the woman said suddenly. "Come heah!"

When he saw that the spotlight was on him at last, Carver drew his feet up and turned himself toward Julian's mother and giggled.

"Carver!" the woman said. "You heah me? Come heah!"

Carver slid down from the seat but remained squatting with his back against the base of it, his head turned slyly around toward Julian's mother, who was smiling at him. The woman reached a hand across the aisle and snatched him to her. He righted himself and hung backwards on her knees, grinning at Julian's mother. "Isn't he cute?" Julian's mother said to the woman with the protruding teeth.

"I reckon he is," the woman said without conviction.

The Negress yanked him upright but he eased out of her grip and shot across the aisle and scrambled, giggling wildly, onto the seat beside his love.

"I think he likes me," Julian's mother said, and smiled at the woman. It was the smile she used when she was being particularly gracious to an inferior. Julian saw everything lost. The lesson had rolled off her like rain on a roof.

The woman stood up and yanked the little boy off the seat as if she were snatching him from contagion. Julian

could feel the rage in her at having no weapon like his
mother's smile. She gave the child a sharp slap across his leg.
He howled once and then thrust his head into her stomach
and kicked his feet against her shins. "Be-have," she said
vehemently.

The bus stopped and the Negro who had been reading the
newspaper got off. The woman moved over and set the little
boy down with a thump between herself and Julian. She held
him firmly by the knee. In a moment he put his hands in
front of his face and peeped at Julian's mother through his
fingers.

"I see yoooooooo!" she said and put her hand in front of
her face and peeped at him.

The woman slapped his hand down. "Quit yo' foolish-
ness," she said, "before I knock the living Jesus out of you!"

Julian was thankful that the next stop was theirs. He
reached up and pulled the cord. The woman reached up and
pulled it at the same time. Oh my God, he thought. He had
the terrible intuition that when they got off the bus together,
his mother would open her purse and give the little boy a
nickel. The gesture would be as natural to her as breathing.
The bus stopped and the woman got up and lunged to the
front, dragging the child, who wished to stay on, after her.
Julian and his mother got up and followed. As they neared
the door, Julian tried to relieve her of her pocketbook.

"No," she murmured, "I want to give the little boy a
nickel."

"No!" Julian hissed. "No!"

She smiled down at the child and opened her bag. The
bus door opened and the woman picked him up by the arm
and descended with him, hanging at her hip. Once in the
street she set him down and shook him.

Julian's mother had to close her purse while she got
down the bus step but as soon as her feet were on the ground,

she opened it again and began to rummage inside. "I can't find but a penny," she whispered, "but it looks like a new one."

"Don't do it!" Julian said fiercely between his teeth. There was a streetlight on the corner and she hurried to get under it so that she could better see into her pocketbook. The woman was heading off rapidly down the street with the child still hanging backward on her hand.

"Oh little boy!" Julian's mother called and took a few quick steps and caught up with them just beyond the lamp-post. "Here's a bright new penny for you," and she held out the coin, which shone bronze in the dim light.

The huge woman turned and for a moment stood, her shoulders lifted and her face frozen with frustrated rage, and stared at Julian's mother. Then all at once she seemed to explode like a piece of machinery that had been given one ounce of pressure too much. Julian saw the black fist swing out with the red pocketbook. He shut his eyes and cringed as he heard the woman shout, "He don't take nobody's pennies!" When he opened his eyes, the woman was disappearing down the street with the little boy staring wide-eyed over her shoulder. Julian's mother was sitting on the sidewalk.

"I told you not to do that," Julian said angrily. "I told you not to do that!"

He stood over her for a minute, gritting his teeth. Her legs were stretched out in front of her and her hat was on her lap. He squatted down and looked her in the face. It was totally expressionless. "You got exactly what you deserved," he said. "Now get up."

He picked up her pocketbook and put what had fallen out back in it. He picked the hat up off her lap. The penny caught his eye on the sidewalk and he picked that up and let it drop before her eyes into the purse. Then he stood up and leaned over and held his hands out to pull her up. She remained immobile. He sighed. Rising above them on either side were black apartment buildings, marked with irregular rectangles of light. At the end of the block a man came out of a door and walked off in the opposite direction. "All right," he said, "suppose somebody happens by and wants to know why you're sitting on the sidewalk?"

She took the hand and, breathing hard, pulled heavily up on it and then stood for a moment, swaying slightly as if the spots of light in the darkness were circling around her. Her eyes, shadowed and confused, finally settled on his face. He did not try to conceal his irritation. "I hope this teaches you a lesson," he said. She leaned forward and her eyes raked his face. She seemed trying to determine his identity. Then, as if she found nothing familiar about him, she started off with a headlong movement in the wrong direction.

"Aren't you going on to the Y?" he asked.

"Home," she muttered.

"Well, are we walking?"

For answer she kept going. Julian followed along, his hands behind him. He saw no reason to let the lesson she had had go without backing it up with an explanation of its meaning. She might as well be made to understand what had happened to her. "Don't think that was just an uppity Negro woman," he said. "That was the whole colored race which will no longer take your condescending pennies. That was your black double. She can wear the same hat as you, and to be sure," he added gratuitously (because he thought it was funny), "it looked better on her than it did on you. What all this means," he said, "is that the old world is gone. The old manners are obsolete and your graciousness is not worth a damn." He thought bitterly of the house that had been lost for him. "You aren't who you think you are," he said.

She continued to plow ahead, paying no attention to him. Her hair had come undone on one side. She dropped her pocketbook and took no notice. He stooped and picked it up and handed it to her but she did not take it.

"You needn't act as if the world had come to an end," he said, "because it hasn't. From now on you've got to live in a new world and face a few realities for a change. Buck up," he said, "it won't kill you."

She was breathing fast.

"Let's wait on the bus," he said.

"Home," she said thickly.

"I hate to see you behave like this," he said. "Just like a child. I should be able to expect more of you." He decided to stop where he was and make her stop and wait for a bus. "I'm not going any farther," he said, stopping. "We're going on the bus."

She continued to go on as if she had not heard him. He took a few steps and caught her arm and stopped her. He looked into her face and caught his breath. He was looking into a face he had never seen before. "Tell Grandpa to come get me," she said.

He stared, stricken.

"Tell Caroline to come get me," she said.

Stunned, he let her go and she lurched forward again, walking as if one leg were shorter than the other. A tide of darkness seemed to be sweeping her from him. "Mother!" he cried. "Darling, sweetheart, wait!" Crumpling, she fell to the pavement. He dashed forward and fell at her side, crying, "Mamma, Mamma!" He turned her over. Her face was fiercely distorted. One eye, large and staring, moved slightly to the left as if it had become unmoored. The other remained fixed on him, raked his face again, found nothing and closed.

"Wait here, wait here!" he cried and jumped up and began to run for help toward a cluster of lights he saw in the distance ahead of him. "Help, help!" he shouted, but his voice was thin, scarcely a thread of sound. The lights drifted farther away the faster he ran and his feet moved numbly as if they carried him nowhere. The tide of darkness seemed to sweep him back to her, postponing from moment to moment his entry into the world of guilt and sorrow.

The March to Montgomery
from From Camelot to Kent State
John Lewis

On February 1, 1965, less than sixty days after winning the Nobel Peace Prize, Dr. Martin Luther King, Jr., was arrested in Selma, Alabama, while campaigning for voting rights for African Americans. On March 21, King led a march from Selma to Montgomery, the state capital. Partly in response to demonstrations like this one, Congress passed the Voting Rights Act in August 1965.

This account of the march to Montgomery is told by one of the leaders, John Lewis, now a congressman from Georgia.

After President Johnson became president, we began to focus on a voter registration bill, because black people were being denied the right to vote or even register to vote in many places in the South, and we had a number of demonstrations in various places. A young black man, who was leading a demonstration near Selma, Alabama, was shot and killed by a state trooper while he was leading a peaceful, orderly, nonviolent march. And we made a decision—Dr. King, Reverend Ralph Abernathy, Andrew Young, and myself—that we should march to Montgomery from Selma to dramatize the need for a voting rights act and to dramatize the violent climate that existed in Alabama.

A day or so before the march was to begin, Governor George Wallace made a statement that it would not be allowed. SNCC debated all night over it. Some were saying that the days of marching were over—someone might get hurt, someone might get killed. But people were coming from all over to join the march, and I felt that if people wanted to march, we should be there with them. Finally, the committee said to me, "You can march as an individual but not as a chairman of SNCC." And I decided to do that.

We met outside the church to participate in the march. We lined up in twos, and Hosea Williams and I were the first two. I don't know what we expected. I think maybe we thought we'd be arrested and jailed or maybe they wouldn't do anything to us. I had a little knapsack on my shoulder with an apple, a toothbrush, toothpaste, and two books in it: a history of America and a book by Thomas Merton.

It was a sunny afternoon. When we got to the top of the bridge crossing the Alabama River, we looked down and we saw this *sea* of blue. It was Alabama state troopers. The night before, Sheriff Clark had asked all white men over the age of twenty-one to come to the Dallas County Courthouse and be deputized to be part of his posse. So they'd all become state troopers. When we looked down, we saw all these men with guns, and we thought, "Well, they're probably going to stop us or arrest us," so we kept on walking.

There was total silence. You could hear only a soft stomp-stomp-stomp of people walking. When we got in hearing distance of the state troopers, a major identified himself and shouted on a bullhorn and said, "This is an unlawful march. It will not be allowed to continue. I give you three minutes to disperse and go back to your church." We kept on walking, and in a very few minutes, less than half a minute maybe, he said, "Troopers advance."

We stopped then. The only thing moving in our line was my trenchcoat flapping back and forth in the wind. I think I said to Hosea something like, "Shall we stand here in a proper manner or shall we kneel?"

But before we could do anything, they came to us—men on horses, men on foot. The horses were trampling over the people, and the state troopers that were not on horses were hitting us with clubs and beating people down with bullwhips. We couldn't go forward, because if you tried to go forward, you were going into the heat of the action. You couldn't go to either side, because you would have been jumping over the bridge into the Alabama River. They came to us as if they were mowing a big field, and they left a path of people lying down on the ground behind them, hollering and screaming.

I was hit in the head, and apparently I blacked out, because I don't know what happened after that. The doctor later said I had a concussion. Someone must have got me back to the church, and I remember saying, "I don't understand how President Johnson can send troops to Vietnam, to the Congo, to Central America, and he can't send troops to protect black people who want the right to register to vote."

The next morning, Dr. King came over to the hospital where I was, and he said something like, "John, don't worry. We're going to make it to Montgomery. I've issued a call for ministers and priests, rabbis and nuns, the religious community of America to come. We're going to make it."

The next day they tried another march, which I couldn't participate in, and several hundred religious leaders got as far as the line of state troopers on the bridge and were turned back. That night the Reverend James Reeb, one of the young white ministers who'd come down, was beaten by a group of white men in Selma. He died a few hours later in a hospital in Birmingham.

Afterward President Johnson went on nationwide television and made what was, to me, the greatest speech ever on the whole question of civil rights. He spoke from the soul about the point in history when fate and time come to a meeting of the ways. He said, "So it was at Lexington and Concord. So it was a century ago at Appomattox. So it was last week in Selma, Alabama." Then he went on to say that the most powerful nation in the world has heard the moan, the groan, the cry of an oppressed people, and we are responding. He said one good man, a man of God, was killed. Two or three times he said there was a need for a strong voting rights bill. At the end he said, "We shall overcome." I saw Dr. King cry that night. Tears came down his cheek, and I knew then that it was just a matter of time till we would have a voting rights act.

Then came the second phase of the march, and it was one of the most meaningful efforts of any demonstration that I participated in. It was black people, it was white people, it was Protestant, it was Jewish, it was Catholic. There were young people, old people, some very poor people, some very rich people, a senator's wife, a cousin of Governor Rockefeller, a former attorney general. People came from all over. They blended together, and we all marched together.

I was still recovering from the concussion, but I marched, too. We had roadside tents along the way for people to stay in, and it took us four or five days to get to Montgomery. We had someone responsible for the preparation of the food, we had trucks to carry the food, and we carried toilets along the way.

President Johnson called out the United States military to protect us, and at night they would shine their huge lights and light up the fields where we were staying. We would see the soldiers on the roadside inspecting the bridges, looking under bridges before we walked across them. It was as if we saw the government of America saying, "These people have a right to exercise their constitutional rights, a right to peaceful protest, to assemble." And President Johnson used the military to make it possible.

Along the way, people made up little songs, marching songs, you know: "Pick 'em up, lay 'em down, all the way from Selma town." There was such a sense of family and sense of community that you sort of wanted to keep on going. There was a sense that we'll get there, we'll make it, because the cause we were involved in was right. It reminded me of Gandhi leading his march to the sea.

The last night we made it to outside Montgomery and gathered together on a grassy field on the campus of Saint Jude's School and Church. There was a huge rally, and people like Harry Belafonte and Joan Baez, Pete Seeger, Peter, Paul, and Mary, and others came and sang with us out in the open, to support our effort.

In the morning, we marched down the streets of Montgomery, up to the steps of the capitol. People kept joining us and by the time we got there we had over thirty thousand people. . . . In October of that year the voting rights bill was passed and we all felt we'd had a part in it.

■ ■ ■